HART CRANE

HART CRANE

A Critical Study

NEIL ROOT

Greenwich Exchange
London

Greenwich Exchange, London

First published in Great Britain in 2025
All rights reserved

Hart Crane: A Critical Study
© Neil Root, 2025

This book is sold subject to the conditions that it shall not, by way of trade or otherwise, be lent, resold, hired out or otherwise circulated without the publisher's prior consent in any form of binding or cover other than that in which it is published and without a similar condition including this condition being imposed on the subsequent purchaser.

Printed and bound by imprintdigital.com
Cover design by December Publications
Tel: 07951511275

Greenwich Exchange Website: www.greenex.co.uk

Cataloguing in Publication Data is available
from the British Library

ISBN: 978-1-910996-79-9

To Matthew Gibson, lover of literature

CONTENTS

Part One *11*

An extended introductory essay introducing Hart Crane (1899-1932) and his poetry, taking in a brief narrative summary of the best criticism from 1926 to date, giving a considered opinion of his oeuvre and legacy.

Part Two *45*

In-depth criticism of a selection of Hart Crane's individual poems and sequences:

From *White Buildings* (1926)

- Legend *47*
- My Grandmother's Love Letters *50*
- Chaplinesque *52*
- At Melville's Tomb *56*
- Voyages I-VI *60*

From *The Bridge* (1930)

- To Brooklyn Bridge *70*
- Ave Maria *72*
- The River *74*
- The Tunnel *79*
- Atlantis *82*

Bibliography

PART ONE
AN EXTENDED INTRODUCTORY ESSAY

IN THE *NEW YORK TIMES* ON 27 April 1930, the reviewer Percy Hutchinson, initialed 'PH', critiqued Hart Crane's freshly published epic poem, made up of fifteen poetic sequences, under the headline 'Hart Crane's cubistic poetry in *The Bridge*'.

One can see how such a labelling could be made, especially at that time, when Cubism, chiefly associated with Picasso, was all the avant-garde rage in Paris, where Crane himself had spent a significant amount of time in the 1920s along with many other expatriate American writers, and where the movement had spread from art and sculpture and seeped into literature and transported that infusion elsewhere.

As the American poet Kenneth Rexroth wrote in his 1969 introduction to the selected poems of the French Cubist poet Pierre Reverdy, in poetry, Cubism, which had a revolutionary impact on traditional painting, 'is the conscious, deliberate dissociation and recombination of elements into a new artistic entity made self-sufficient by its rigorous architecture.' Crane certainly played with form and juxtaposition of both traditional and modernist poetic influences and elements, but there was always a formal structure, or what Rexroth calls 'architecture' to his poetry.

Crane is often seen as a seer, a visionary, and that's also easily explained. Like all the greatest poets, he makes you both think and feel. At his best, he was capable of the purest searing lyricism conveying a deep empathy for the human condition, tempered by gritty realism through his depiction of what he saw directly around him, a profound intellectual understanding of myth through metaphor, and, mainlined from his heart, Crane's verse stabs at you with piercingly acute and exhilarating emotion.

So, Crane has structure and form, as well as a very receptive eye and ear. In fact, it can be argued that the latter – Crane's ear – is one of his strongest attributes. The rhythms and cadences of his best poems and sequences are mesmerising, and draw you in, with a real feeling of music and composition. To make such music with words is a difficult feat. To take two of Crane's known literary influences as examples, James Joyce could do it in prose, and T.S. Eliot, in poetry. So could Crane, and once he had managed to extricate himself from Eliot's hold enough to form his own voice, Crane made words sing.

Like most poetry of the highest calibre, the poet's life is inextricably and understandably linked to the poems. Poetry is the most intimate form of writing, requiring a huge concentration of power and meaning, every word truly having to earn its place and position in a line, and first-rank poets who explore the human condition have no choice but to spill or pour a great deal of themselves onto the page.

The poet Robert Lowell's celebrated 1959 poem 'Words for Hart Crane' elegantly and pointedly touches on many seminal angles of Crane's life and work. Lowell recognised both Crane's sometimes taxing intellectual profundity, and his ability to fire arrows into the reader's heart: 'Who asks for me, the Shelley of my age, must lay his heart out for my bed and board.' You need to earn your place at Crane's poetic feast.

The rest of Lowell's poem reminds us that Crane never got the financial stability his ambitions expected, and his full critical due, during his short lifetime, outside of a small circle of fellow poets. He was largely seen as at best a 'nearly great' by the wider literary establishment, and a self-indulgent and unrestrained poet without a defined subject at worst, although a small group of esteemed dramatists, novelists, and critics valued him highly.

And Lowell also reminds us how well-read Crane was, as he channels him, almost thirty years after his death – 'Because I knew my Whitman like a book.' The fact that Crane really 'knew' his literature is something attested to by many of his close friends and confidants, such as the novelist and critic Waldo Frank, the critic Gorham Munson, the critic and poet Malcolm Cowley, and the bookseller Samuel Loveman. The latter of whom, driven by sporadic impecunity, was later revealed to be a forger of signed bibliographic artefacts, including some by Crane.

But the most revealing observation that Lowell makes about Crane in his poem comes in the line 'stranger in America', as that goes to the root of who Crane was, through his sensitive temperament; sexuality at that unforgivingly homophobic time, even though he was openly gay by the standards of that era, and, as Lowell makes clear, almost predatory at times; and perhaps most heart-breaking for Crane – a man whom Cowley once said was 'an artist to his fingertips' – his talent.

Crane, through his stubborn and uncompromising artistic temperament – although he did make attempts at normal employment alongside writing his poetry – ultimately refused to meet halfway a world which has often undervalued its true artists. And in the 1920s when Crane did the vast bulk of his writing, capitalism was king, especially in New York where Crane lived for most of that decade, at least until the Wall Street Crash of late 1929 ushered in its swiftly entrenched societal aftershocks.

The cold and hostile Great Depression-era New York that Crane feared returning to, broke once again, in 1932, after his Guggenheim-funded year in Mexico, creatively blocked and unfulfilled, surely must have been a factor in his sense of desperate hopelessness, in what was certainly his suicide on the way back. Being a poet was his entire raison d'être and identity, whether self-constructed or by calling, depending on your point of view, and the very essence of who he was must have seemed lost.

And two years earlier, the last sentence of that 1930 on-publication-review of *The Bridge* in the *New York Times* must have been deeply wounding for Crane. 'In spite of its glitter and its seeming intellectual importance, a piece that is in the main spurious as poetry,' the review concluded. He had laboured for years on that work, and he was always in need of validation, in between bouts of euphoric roaring, undoubtedly exacerbated by alcohol, and perhaps manic depression or bipolar disorder, then commonly known as 'mania'.

You can be a long-term admirer of Crane's poetry and see him as one of the handful of truly major twentieth-century poets as many, although far from all, do, and still recognise his deficiencies. Crane was a complex and troubled man, and his work is extremely demanding of both reader focus, indeed perseverance, and time.

Self-indulgent obscurity is a charge often made against Crane, especially in his later poetry between 1927 and 1932 – some sections of *The Bridge*, the posthumously published *Key West: An Island Sheaf*, and *The Broken* Tower. The poems in his earlier collection *White Buildings* – published in 1926 as a book collection, but some appeared in magazines and journals earlier – are generally more readily accessible.

Crane can be highly obscure, sometimes seemingly willfully so, as if his lines and word choices are a Matryoshka or Russian doll, which we must continuously dive deeper into and unbox to fathom core and intended meaning. And on occasion, even as a committed devotee of Crane's poetry, you can wonder if there is any true meaning behind those words at all, especially when you read that according to his close friend the painter Charmion von Wiegand, as a young man Crane would obsessively read a thesaurus.

Other modern poets have been accused of style – for effect – over substance, such as Dylan Thomas, whose sonorous rhetoric can lift and move you, but then leave you wondering why, and what those elegiac words really mean. And this criticism can certainly be levelled at Crane – his word choices are rarely straightforward, often opaque, and while they provide rich layering, are often confusing and disturb flow of thought and comprehension.

The then very influential critic Edmund Wilson, writing in the *New Republic* after Crane's first collection *White Buildings* appeared in 1926, recognised the poet's beautiful style, but was critical of the substance of the poems: 'Though he can sometimes move us, the emotion is oddly vague', and that while Crane has 'a style that is strikingly original – almost something like a great style, if there could be such a thing as a great style ... (It is) not ... applied to any subject at all.'

It would only be decades later, especially by critics focusing on Crane's sexuality, and his work read in a gay subtext, that his opaqueness and lack of accessible and easily definable meaning would be seen as a smokescreen of the poet's reality in his lifetime: expressing his innermost thoughts and feelings, but in an often-guarded way, as a shield. But that again can be a disservice to Crane's poetic achievement – the fact that he was gay is intrinsic to who he was and therefore his work, but his poetry can be read, digested, and enjoyed without limiting him to the tunnel of sexuality, just as Auden, another major gay poet, can be read on several levels.

Perhaps the best explanation of Hart Crane's poetic sensibility came from the poet himself, when in 1926, he wrote to Harriet Monroe, influential editor of *Poetry* magazine in Chicago, who like Edmund Wilson, questioned the lack of a coherent subject and coherent meaning in Crane's poetry. She had received his poem 'At Melville's Tomb', which was included in *White Buildings*, but complained about its obscurity, and said that she would publish it, but that Crane would have to provide some exposition of the poem for readers. 'At Melville's Tomb' is examined in Part Two of this study.

Crane's letter to Monroe in riposte, which was published in *Poetry* in October 1926, is worth quoting at length to understand the philosophy behind his poetics.

'This may sound as though I merely fancied juggling words and images until I found something novel, or esoteric; but the process is much more predetermined and objectified than that. The nuances and feeling and observation in a poem may well call for certain liberties which you claim the poet has no right to take. ('Hart Crane: A Letter to Harriet Monroe', *Modern American Poetry*). I am simply making the claim that the poet does have that authority, and that to deny it is to limit the scope of the medium so considerably as to outlaw some of the richest genius of the past ... emotional dynamics are not to be confused with any absolute order of rationalized definitions; ergo, in poetry the rationale of metaphor belongs to another order of experience than science and is not to be limited by a scientific and arbitrary code or relationships either in verbal inflections or concepts.'

This shows us that Crane's poetry is considered and has a very keen literary brain behind it, as well as the obvious great lyrical talent. It also shows that Crane himself demanded, and expected, intellectual vigour in the reading of his poetry. For this reason, it could be said that the final line in the aforementioned poem 'Words for Hart Crane' by Robert Lowell should be amended to, 'Who asks for me ... must lay his heart *and mind* out for his bed and board.'

Many poets and critics, in Crane's lifetime, and in the decades after Crane's death – some of whom knew him, such as Yvor Winters and Allen Tate – still questioned the 'substance' of Crane's work, and while they saw that he possessed great poetic powers, many felt that he failed to capitalise on them, even wasted them. Harold Bloom was a high-profile exception and saw Crane as 'the most ambitious of American poets', and Crane moved Bloom more than any other poet.

And how many poets managed to write poems of the magnitude of some in *White Buildings* and *The Bridge*? No more than a handful in the twentieth century. It recalls the riposte given by the novelist Joseph Heller when somebody once asked him why he hadn't written anything as good as *Catch-22* since. 'Who has?' he said.

Serious readers of Crane's poetry really do have to work hard – to truly access him takes deep thinking, literary knowledge, a love for, and curiosity about, language, and increasingly as the decades pass – Crane's last published poetry is approaching its centenary – social and historical context. There are a handful of poems which can be read and enjoyed on an epidermis level, but to make and get the most out of Crane requires dedication, a plunging beneath that surface covering of rich words placed in a lyrical order.

And then come the real rewards: a grasp of Crane's fine intellect; literary nous – his voracious reading was fostered and enabled as a child by his beloved grandmother's extensive library; acute ambition – nobody could ever accuse Crane of not stretching himself; self-awareness of his place within the literary tradition; and a self-conscious desire to become part of the canon. For Crane was in fact a traditionalist, and heavily influenced by the French Symbolists, such as Arthur Rimbaud, Charles Baudelaire, Guillaume Apollinaire, Tristan Corbière, Paul Valéry, and like T.S. Eliot famously, Jules Laforgue.

Running roughly from 1840 to 1920, the Symbolism movement is now widely seen as the poetic bridge between Romanticism and Modernism, so its period was ending just as Crane was seriously sharpening his pencils and changing his typewriter ribbon with intent.

In addition, homegrown literary influences deeply impacted Crane: the seminal American poet Walt Whitman – like Crane, a gay man who had expressed himself freely in his work in a world which frowned upon his sexuality – and the American essayist and poet Ralph Waldo Emerson. Whitman especially, who was both a follower of the liberal and progressive American early nineteenth-century Transcendentalism philosophy (the belief that there is inherent goodness in all people and nature), and a realist, has often been cited as Crane's great poetic forebear.

With his definitive 1855 collection *Leaves of Grass*, Whitman celebrated America (as well as himself) in free verse, and Crane's great project *The Bridge* also aimed to explore America through myth and the past. And Crane quoted lines from Whitman's poem 'A Passage to India' to preface the 'Cape Hatteras' section of *The Bridge*, which ends 'My hand/ in yours,/Walt Whitman – /so – ' Revealingly, Crane also quoted Seneca, Plato, Melville, Marlowe, Emily Dickinson, and William Blake at the beginning of other sequences of that poem.

But Crane also owed a large debt to the English Romantic poetic tradition, from the Elizabethans: Christopher Marlowe, Shakespeare, and John Donne, in the late sixteenth and early seventeenth centuries, through to Coleridge, Shelley, Keats, Robert Browning, and Gerard Manley Hopkins, from the late eighteenth, and early, mid, and late nineteenth centuries.

We can see the imprint of both the Elizabethans and the French Symbolists in Crane's first collection, *White Buildings* (1926). And these influences continue to vein through *The Bridge* (1930), although by this time Crane's voice was more his own. But Crane of course wasn't the first to connect these two literary strands – in fact, T.S. Eliot, American by birth and exiled in Britain by choice, was the major poet who fused them together, in his early major poems such as 'The Love Song of J. Alfred Prufrock' and 'Preludes', and of course *The Waste Land*.

Hart Crane was twenty-three when *The Waste Land* appeared in 1922, the same year in which James Joyce's *Ulysses* was thrust upon the world, Eliot and Joyce heralding in the era of Modernism in poetry and prose respectively. And like every other poet of the next twenty years, at least until Auden took verse in a new direction in the mid to late 1930s, Eliot was the poetic gold standard. Budding poets had to read him, absorb him, emulate him, and for those desperate to be more than journeymen or journeywomen and to find their own voice, escape his omnipresent, looming shadow.

As the critic Ian Hamilton wrote in his book *Against Oblivion: Some Lives of the Twentieth-Century Poets*, 'Every

Anglo-American poet who postdated Eliot was haunted by *The Waste Land.*' And Crane, like all the poets of the interwar years with a serious vocation and ambition, had to crawl out from under Eliot's heavy poetic rock, the opposite of Eliot telling readers of *The Waste Land* to 'Come in under the shadow of this red rock.'

And a reading of Crane's letters shows many references to Eliot, Ezra Pound, and the Elizabethans. For instance, as early as November 1919, when Crane was twenty, and *The Waste Land* was almost three years away from changing the English-speaking poetic landscape, he wrote to his friend Gorham Munson: 'More and more I am turning towards Pound and Eliot and the minor Elizabethans for values.'

Crane managed, to some extent, to break free of Eliot, in terms of style, but not in terms of the need to attempt a long thematic poem, which would culminate in *The Bridge.* Although he was able to extricate himself from Eliot's bleakly negative view of the spiritual state of humanity after the First World War.

But a letter from Crane to his friend the poet and critic Allen Tate in May 1922, reveals that Crane was trying to move away from a negative tone in his poetry before *The Waste Land.* 'The poetry of negation is beautiful – alas too dangerously so for one of my mind. But I am trying to break away from it.' That was written five months before *The Waste Land* first appeared in *The Criterion* magazine in Britain and six months before it was published in *The Dial* in America.

As for forming his own style, Brom Weber, later the editor of Crane's 1966 *Complete Poems, Selected Prose and Letters,* wrote in a 1935 essay about Crane: 'The form which Crane took as he shook free from the spirit of Eliot was the blank verse which had been brilliantly employed by Eliot and Wallace Stevens, and before them by the Elizabethans.'

Crane immersed himself in Eliot, and Crane would have read poems such as 'The Comedian as the Letter C', from Stevens's 1923 first collection *Harmonium* – Crane recommended Stevens to friends before that book appeared. Like those poets, Crane saw the potential of blank verse – iambic pentameter which is unrhymed – and, imperatively, made the form his own.

But Crane also read the Elizabethan originals, and his letters show that Marlowe deeply affected him. The metre suited Crane, as Brom Weber wrote, as 'In blank verse there was a measure of metrical discipline, but it could be balanced with run-on lines and verbal variations in sufficient quantity to provide a field of activity for musical exuberance ... '

But did Crane comprehensively break free from Eliot's influence? The answer must be no.

In his short lifetime, Crane never truly liberated himself from Eliot in terms of technique – the use of Elizabethan blank verse and the stamp of the French Symbolists, both present in Eliot; or subject matter – the drive to write a culturally defining long poem, as Eliot had achieved with *The Waste Land*. But poems which appeared posthumously, such as the ones in *Key West: An Island Sheaf*, and *The Broken Tower*, show that Crane was still developing, and it's exciting to imagine where he would have gone and arrived at in terms of style and subject matter, even if he felt creatively wrung out at the time of his death.

However, in *The Bridge*, Crane was able to forge his own

optimistic, often joyous vision, using a centuries-old poetic metre to fit his requirements in the High Modernist era.

And in that long poem, the work for which Crane is now certainly most known, he created his own juxtaposition of America's past and present, myth and reality. In his own unique poetic voice, which was infused with sweat, fear, identity, insecurity (both as an artist in a pounding capitalist world, and sexually), ecstasy, and tears. And the copious amounts of alcohol he drank wasn't obviously spilt to create the revelry, and occasionally orgasmic and revelatory lyricism he produced on the page.

*

So, what about the man?

Writing poetry of the intensity achieved by Hart Crane requires deep introspection, a mining of the soul, as well as mind, and so, a lot of himself went into his poems. The work of too many poets, Crane being a prominent example, has often been overshadowed by their lives, with biographies receiving far more attention than the poetry itself. But to really understand Crane poems, the reader does need to explore what drove him during his lifetime.

It's no coincidence that Robert Lowell, the first top-rank twentieth-century poet to (self-) consciously and persistently plunder and air his troubled inner psyche in his work, almost three decades after Crane's death in *Life Studies*, felt an affinity with Crane, and saw his true worth.

And the lineage went on – Lowell the father of the 'Confessional' school of poetry, directly influenced his contemporary John Berryman, and his students, the younger poets Anne Sexton and Sylvia Plath, to put their inner thoughts and demons into their work, through the 1960s and into the early 1970s, forty years after Crane's death.

Crane cannot be seen as a confessional poet in the way Lowell and the poets mentioned above were, but his soul-and-heart-searching, rumination, and meditation to pull the words and themes out of himself during periods of composition, a turning in on himself, was unusual during his lifetime. Even though Coleridge, a known influence on Crane, was doing just that over a century earlier – in fact, Coleridge died ninety-eight years before Crane. Crane's stimulant was alcohol, whereas Coleridge's was opium.

Crane's biggest contemporary influence, T.S. Eliot, had elements of himself in his poetry, but he was obscured, austere, and removed in his early work published during Crane's lifetime, and his major theme was spiritual struggle. It was only in *Four Quartets*, the first section of which, 'Burnt Norton', was published four years after Crane died, and six years after *The Bridge* appeared, where Eliot began to show himself more. But Crane's earlier collection, *White Buildings*, was also deeply personal in matter and manner, as we shall see, addressing his sexuality, his place in the world, his family, just as Lowell would do later in *Life Studies*.

Crane is often seen as a poet who lets his emotions run unleashed, creating an unfettered maelstrom, but there is an ordered intellect behind that emotion. That battle between the mind and heart lies at the centre of Crane's life, as well as his deeply personal poetry. This tussling is especially apparent in *The Bridge*, a long poem which requires architecture, where he attempted the considerable feat of melding an overarching themed structure to his flights of aroused imagination in accumulative sequences.

Harold (Hart) Crane wasn't a native metropolitan New Yorker at all. But that city, along with to a lesser extent, Cuba, and Mexico, most inspired him. He was born on 21 July 1899, in Garrettsville, Ohio, a village, which in the 1900 census had a population of 1,145, and even in 2010, still only had 2,325 residents.

And at the beginning of the twentieth century, the Crane family was the most prominent in Garrettsville. This was because it was, at that time, the place where the most maple syrup was processed in the world, and this was due to Hart Crane's grandfather Arthur Crane, who had begun to can maple syrup for manufacture in the late nineteenth century.

So, Hart's father Clarence, or 'C.A.' Crane, was an important man locally, and he married Grace Edna Hart in Garrettsville on 1 June 1898, just over a year before the future poet's arrival. But Hart wouldn't stay in Garrettsville for too long, for when he was just ten years old in 1909 his parents relocated to the city of Cleveland. C.A. continued his confectionery or 'candy' business there, and in 1911 changed his focus from his own father's maple syrup mainstay to the production of chocolates.

That was what led C.A. in 1912 to invent a sweet which remains a mainstay of American candy to this day – the ring-shaped Life Saver (it's now produced by Wrigley in the US and Nestlé in Canada). An astute businessperson, C.A. came up with the idea to give him 'summer candy' to sell – chocolate sales tended to dip due to the heat at that time of the year, as it melted. But not so astutely with the unfair benefit of hindsight, C.A. sold his rights to the brand in 1913, for the then substantial sum of $2,900, but a pittance compared to what it would later be worth.

Still, C.A. was a hard-headed businessman, and his inability to understand his only child's deepfelt vocation as a poet from his mid-teens, a conflict and lack of mutual empathy between son and father was inevitable. For a time, C.A humoured Hart's ambition to an extent, and tried to help in his own way. C.A. was always willing to have Hart come home to work in his factory when times just became too tough, but with his own underlying agenda – the hope that his son would take to the business world and make a long-term go of it.

In fact, Hart did enjoy working with his father's employees, and being around machines, but his calling as a poet meant his creative spirit was ever restless and he always wanted to be where there was action. New York and its upstate suburbs, where almost all of his artistic and intellectual friends lived, repeatedly pulled him back.

C.A. never understood or showed Hart the encouragement and validation he needed in his art, and the proudest he ever was of Hart was when the leading New York investment banker Otto Kahn became Hart's financial backer, enabling him to concentrate fully on his writing, for a spell. Hart had written begging letters to several millionaires, and Kahn responded. It helped that literary luminaries such as Eugene O'Neill and Sherwood Anderson were talking up Crane's talent at around that time.

Kahn was a lover of the arts – he was chair of the Metropolitan

Opera, and at various times also the patron of the composer George Gershwin, the film director Sergei Eisenstein, and the conductor Arturo Toscanini. The $2,000 that Kahn gave Crane in instalments while he was writing *The Bridge* – apparently as a 'loan', but which he never really expected back – wasn't repaid. Kahn, a titan of the financial world and business pages, was once on the cover of *Time* magazine and known as the 'King of New York,' and Mammon's seal of approval temporarily got C.A.'s attention.

C.A. and Hart's mother Grace divorced in 1917, the year that Hart turned eighteen, and when he first went to New York, initially funded by C.A. As Crane's forensic biographer John Unterecker reveals in his 1969 biography *Voyager*, a book which is important as it has first-hand interviews with many who knew Crane personally, Hart's parents had a difficult and disagreeable marriage. This undoubtedly had a profound effect on the sensitive Hart, and while he had little in common with his father, his mother would often denigrate his father to bring Hart closer to her side, especially in her letters to him.

C.A. died just nine-and-a-half months before Hart, and by then father and son had become estranged. And the same was true with Grace – Hart became estranged from her in 1928. Hart was far closer to her than C.A., and she loved him deeply. But she was also domineering and smothered him, and for Hart, who couldn't bear to feel trapped, that was untenable for any length of time. Crane's friend Samuel Loveman, who had known Hart and his parents in Cleveland, before, like Hart, he migrated to New York, later said that it was very sad that Crane's relationship with both his parents, especially with his mother, broke down.

Hart's conflicting and troubled emotions about his relationships with both parents seem to have been a key factor in Hart's ultimate emotional unravelling. Hart was also very close to his grandmother, Elizabeth Hart, and this will be explored later in this study, in Part Two, when his poem 'My Grandmother's Love Letters' is examined. Elizabeth died in 1928, while Hart was working on *The Bridge*. She was undoubtedly an emotionally stabilizing factor in Hart's life – they wrote to each other often – and her passing must have left a void. And Hart needed stability, as he was, just as Lowell wrote, 'a stranger in America', an unanchored outsider on three levels.

As with some other 'born' writers, Hart's purely felt sense of calling as a poet meant that he struggled to engage with the real world, much more than many of his contemporaries. He was often self-indulgent and demanding, as if the world owed him a living. This could lead to tantrums, and while he could be a very loyal, good friend, he would sometimes take his friends for granted and treat them badly.

Secondly, Hart was a boy from the provinces, somewhat lost in New York as a young man – the bright lights and artistic stimulation of the great metropolis both thrilled him and exacerbated his impecunity, made worse by his almost certain alcoholism, although he could remain sober for stretches when focused and working intensely. And thirdly, his sexuality must have made him feel different on a primal level, like many others in the society of that time.

But at a time when being gay was shunned and stigmatised,

gay sex highly illegal, and the vast majority of gay men were forced to remain safely, if often painfully, 'in the closet', Hart was far more open than most.

Most of Hart's love affairs were short, and his affections were often unreciprocated. This wasn't helped by the fact that Hart had an often-risky penchant for what would later be called 'rough trade', and Hart especially liked sailors. In fact, shortly before his death by suicide on a ship in the Gulf of Mexico in April 1932, he had been beaten up by a sailor whom he had propositioned aboard.

So, there was certainly a predatory aspect to Hart's search for fast sexual gratification, and the legal (arrest) and physical dangers (he was 'rolled' more than once) were always lurking, whether in New York, or Paris, where he spent his grandmother's inheritance in late 1928 and early 1929, or on his final seabound journey.

But Hart was also looking for love, and when these brief affairs broke down, he was sometimes thrust into emotional turmoil. In late 1923, Hart fell in love with Emil Opffer, a Norwegian sailor, and by all accounts Emil was the love of his life, although it would eventually, like all the other liaisons, end. The relationship with Opffer was a very significant one in the poet's life, however, and inspired the 'Voyages' sequence of poems which appeared in *White Buildings*, and these poems are examined in Part Two of this study.

Hart is often said to have been openly gay, as his poetic predecessor Walt Whitman had been decades earlier, and Hart was to an extent – amongst his small circle of close friends, although he may not have directly spoken about it. But we know that neither of his parents ever acknowledged it – his clinging and controlling mother Grace certainly knew, and his father C.A. almost definitely did too but chose to ignore it. And as the critic Edward Halsey Foster wrote in 2017, 'Homosexual writers in the 1920s and 1930s, such as Hart Crane, avoided public expression of their sexuality.'

At the end of his life, Hart had his only known love affair with a woman, Peggy Baird, then married to his friend, the poet and critic Malcolm Cowley. He spent his last days with her in Mexico, and he was travelling back to New York with her on a ship at the time of his death. And it is well-documented that Hart questioned whether he had ever really been gay and believed that he was truly in love with her. This surely shows that Hart was less than secure in his sexuality, even in the last months of his life.

All of this must have worked its way into the poetry, for even if Hart never overtly addressed his own sexuality, it's there in the subtext and in a close reading of many of his poems, as is so much of this poet. For as stated earlier, Hart Crane was a complex person, and his poetry mirrors that complexity of thought and feeling.

*

The arsenic suicide of the penniless and despondent 17-year-old poet and forger Thomas Chatterton in Holborn, London in 1770 heavily influenced the mindset and myth which built around the Romantics, of the following two generations – Wordsworth, Coleridge, Keats, Shelley, and Byron – particularly the latter three, who all suffered early demises. And this fascination with death over life grew during the twentieth century. The tragic deaths of poets – although in the case of the

American poet Weldon Kees, a disappearance presumed suicide – have threatened to overshadow the poetry they wrote while they lived and breathed.

Hart Crane, along with fellow American poets who took their own lives early, such as Sylvia Plath, Anne Sexton, John Berryman, and Delmore Schwartz, (who died of natural causes, but living a seedy hermit existence in a hotel room while mentally unwell), are prime examples of this inclination, which could be called the curse of the death cult. All have their deaths prominently mentioned when they appear in anthologies, criticism, or in the mainstream media, and their biographies tend to focus on the tragedy of their demise.

It is also notable that the common denominator here, as well as being poets, is that they were all American. The nineteenth-century English fixation with literary tragic death made its way across the Atlantic and flourished there by the mid-late twentieth century. Or more likely it's purely a dark human impulse, and poets attract death worship as they explore the human condition, both the lightness and the darkness of being alive, in their work. As in crime writing, it seems often in literature, 'If it bleeds it leads'.

Icons in other mediums, such as Rudolph Valentino, Marilyn Monroe, and James Dean in film, or the so-called '27 Club' in rock music – the strange number of musicians of the 1960s and 1970s who died at that age – have, of course, suffered the same fate of a macabrely shrouded legacy. But the seeds of the death cult phenomenon germinated in poetry, and memoirists, biographers, newspapers, film and television, websites, and social media continue to keep it fertile to this day.

If Crane had not, in a willful, premeditated gesture, neatly folded his overcoat over the deck railing on the steamship Orizaba and jumped overboard just before midday on 27 April 1932, there's no telling what his legacy would be now. Would it be enhanced or diminished?

There is no doubt that Crane's work has, to an extent, profited from the interest in his suicide, as that has meant more media interest in him. And as recently as 2011, the American actor James Franco starred in, and directed, a biographical film about Crane, *The Broken Tower*, the title taken from the 1932 Crane poem of the same name.

Co-written by Franco and Crane's biographer Paul Mariani, it's a noble, if slightly pretentious attempt to understand Crane. It promisingly takes the 'Voyages' poems of Crane as 'chapters' within the film, and Franco does read some of the poetry. But the focus of the film is squarely on an earlier suicide attempt by Crane, his sexuality, difficulties adapting to conventional employment, alcoholism, and eventual suicide. Franco himself said publicly that he was attracted to the material by the tragedy of Crane's life.

Crane's first biographer John Unterecker in 1969's *Voyager: A Life of Hart Crane* gives us an extremely detailed overview of Crane's life and the composition of his poetry during it, in its close to 800 pages. This is the best reference to Crane's overall life, but it does not address his sexuality in any depth, as it is very conservative in tone, and due to when it was written, there is little analysis of the fact that Hart was gay at all. More recent biographers, such as Paul Mariani with *The Broken Tower* (2000) and Clive Fisher's *Hart Crane: A Life* (2002) both add more, especially about Crane's tumultuous sexual/love life, but the focus is ultimately on Crane as a tragic figure.

Suicide is almost always a tragic final act, especially when young, so no biography could truthfully give Crane's life, in its finality, an upward trajectory. On the other hand, none of them have managed to capture the beauty and euphoria of his verse either. Only the poetry can do that, so the important task is to encourage readers to engage with it, as that is the true and purest heartfelt and mindful essence of Hart Crane. What matters is to get past his life and experience his life's work.

The prevailing image of Crane in the media, and one which has attached to him over time, fueled by his suicide at the age of thirty-two is: the despondent, misunderstood, and failed gay poet who both romantically and tragically opted out of the cruel, unforgiving world into which he didn't fit. Many who haven't read the poetry and experienced the greatness and near-greatness of much of it, are left seeing him as an interesting footnote – a minor cultural Jazz Age icon for the most, and a ready-made martyr both for some in the gay community, and for those who like their poets to demonstratively suffer for their art.

In prose writing, a similar death cult whirls around F. Scott Fitzgerald, the victim of a fatal heart attack at forty-four, when he was hardly selling, and was seen as a drunken has-been in literary circles. But the deserved and later acceptance of *The Great Gatsby* as a masterpiece of American literature keeps recognition and reverence of Fitzgerald's achievement alive in the mainstream, just as T.S. Eliot remains positioned in the cultural gods with *The Waste Land*. Both works defined their culture and so remain set in the granite of the literary pantheon of the 1920s – *The Great Gatsby* as a parable of the American Dream, and *The Waste Land* as a crying out against the spiritual decline and desolation after the First World War.

This is what Hart Crane lacks, a single work that defines his epoch succinctly. He published only two books of poetry in his lifetime of course, and it is his second, *The Bridge*, which defines him. And that, as we have discussed, was inspired by Eliot, as many poets continued to be for some time, including the Bollingen Prize-winning Delmore Schwartz, with his poorly received long poem *Genesis*, which was published two decades after Eliot's magnum opus appeared, in 1943.

The Bridge was an extremely ambitious project, to capture the myth of America through its many-tentacled origins and history up to the neon-lit 1920s. The long poem is now broadly regarded as a glorious failure, a noble undertaking, but one with which Crane overstretched himself and his talent. But did he? It doesn't have the same cohesion and compactness as *The Waste Land*, but then Crane didn't have Ezra Pound as his editor, whom even Eliot acknowledged was '*il miglior fabbro*' (the superior/better craftsman), referencing Dante in his poem's dedication to Pound, who even renamed the poem from Eliot's less epochal 'He Do the Police in Different Voices'.

And Crane does not have Eliot's, or indeed Fitzgerald's cultural warning in *The Bridge*, which is a celebration of America, where it came from, and where it was at the time of its writing. Perhaps that is another reason for its failure to stand as a major and successful milestone in the canon – it doesn't have a bleak diagnosis of society at its core, but an exposition of a country and culture, its history, and values.

Crane pulled no proverbial punches, and wrote what he saw and felt, aided by what his biographer John Unterecker calls an 'extensive reading program' during periods of its long composition. But *The Bridge* is no rallying cry to recognise societal ills. And in the early twentieth century, serious literature in English, both in poetry and prose, was about asking questions and raising awareness of the problems facing human beings and how they lived.

The quality of the writing in Crane's work, in *The Bridge*, *White Buildings*, and his last poems, cannot be in doubt, by any measure of literary merit. At their best, the lyricism soars, and the sequences drive the reader, taking you on a unique and all-encompassing journey, arguably no less and even more than Eliot manages for any sustained length of time.

Many have complained that the disparity between Crane's best and worst work is too great, more so than most poets of the first rank. But Crane came the closest to Eliot in achieving a great long poem in the twentieth century with *The Bridge*, Pound's *Cantos* and Berryman's *Dream Songs* being quite different works, as these long sequences were added to sporadically over a long period of time.

Hart Crane therefore deserves to be rescued from the cult of death lens through which he is viewed by many. His eventful life will undoubtedly always be entwined with his work to an extent, but his death by his own hand shouldn't define that intricate and beautiful work. Crane is worth much more than that, and he repays careful and immersive reading with true and lasting literary reward, reminding you along the way that you are witnessing a natural genius at work, and one who intrinsically cared about his artistry and craft.

But like many great writers, Crane's talents defy definitive analysis. Crane was a natural poet, with a unique voice. As the revered critic of American literature and Shakespeare Harold Bloom wrote, 'Like Milton, Pope, and Tennyson, the youthful Crane was a consecrated poet before he was an adolescent.'

Hart Crane worked hard on his poetry, and on his wide reading, but he already had the innate raw material within him, through mind and temperament, to write poems of a very high, and sometimes of the very highest, calibre.

*

Hart Crane's poetry certainly hasn't been neglected critically – in fact, the analysis has been lengthy and wide in focus. To put Crane's work into critical context before an examination is made of individual poems and sequences in Part Two of this study, a summary of the gist of the most important criticism follows.

The first serious criticism of Crane's work was the already noted critic and later poet Allen Tate's introduction to Crane's first book, *White Buildings*, in 1926. Tate opened his short essay with grand praise: 'The poetry of Hart Crane is ambitious. It is the only poetry I am acquainted with that is at once contemporary and in the grand manner. It is an American poetry.'

But, although Tate was Crane's friend, he was also measured

in his reading of the poetry, and towards the end of his essay, expressed his reservations. 'His faults ... lie in the occasional failure of meeting between vision and subject ... The vision often strains and overreaches the theme.' This is exactly the criticism that Edmund Wilson and Harriet Monroe would soon make about Crane's first collection, and one wonders if they were taking Tate's reading as their lead.

But Tate went on to state in his introduction that it was 'common amongst ambitious poets since Baudelaire' to have stronger imagery than subject, in effect style over substance, and that 'it appears whenever the existing poetic order no longer supports the imagination. It appeared in the eighteenth-century poetry of William Blake.'

Tate, himself yet to publish his own first collection, which would appear two years later and include his most famous poem, 'Ode to the Confederate Dead', gives his fellow young poet – he and Crane were exact contemporaries – some critical leeway, but the charge of style over substance/subject continues to dog Crane for many discerning readers, and there is sometimes real justification for it.

In an essay entitled 'The Progress of Hart Crane' published in *Poetry* magazine in June 1930 when Crane was alive, another of Crane's friends, the poet and critic Yvor Winters, took him to task on the same perceived fault in his poetry. Published several months after the publication of Crane's second book, filled entirely by the sequences of his long poem *The Bridge*, Winters, who two decades later would be very influential and act as a mentor to another powerful, gay poet, Thom Gunn, made his feelings plain. Winters opined that while he could achieve moments of exultation, Crane displayed a lack of control in *The Bridge*:

> Hypnosis is achieved, and lines of pure electricity occur ... The poem is composed mainly of unfused details and is excited rather than rhythmic. The quality which we call restraint, and which is here lacking, is a result of the feeling on the part of a poet that the motivation of his emotion of sound and needs no justification, that the emotion is inevitable; his problem then, is only to give order to his emotion. In Mr Crane we see an attempt to emotionalize a theme to the point where both he and the reader will forget to question its justification ... its low spots are imprecise – in place of exact description we get vague thunder.

This criticism of Crane is, as it had been since 1926, the main charge made against him, as discussed earlier: style over substance, emotion over order, form over content, poetry for effect. There is truth in this, and Crane can freewheel with his emotions at times, with no attempt at reining in as can be seen in the more controlled poetry of his own peers and near-contemporaries, the considered, careful, and revered Eliot a prime example, who allowed us just a glimpse of his emotion while espousing his clear themes. But to say that Crane lacks a rhythmic quality in his work is unfair, and this will be discussed in more detail in Part Two.

Winters had been a qualified but cautiously enthusiastic admirer of the poems in *White Buildings*, published four years earlier, and in his conclusion, he makes his view clear that Crane had taken a wrong turn with *The Bridge* and the feeling that the poet was too heavily influenced by the sonorous poetry of Walt Whitman. 'It is possible that Mr Crane may recover himself. In any event, he has given us, in his first book (*White Buildings*) several lyrics that one is tempted to call great, and in both books (alongside *The Bridge*) several charming minor lyrics and many magnificent fragments. And one thing he has demonstrated, the impossibility of getting anywhere with the Whitmanian inspiration.'

One of Crane's closest friends, the critic and novelist Waldo Frank, who would do much over the next decades to resurrect Crane critically, was more positive about *The Bridge* in a 1933 essay, a year after Crane's death. Firstly, he rhapsodises about Crane's lyricism, which, to be fair, almost all critics valued. 'The beauty of Crane's lyrics, and of many passages ... seems to me to be inviolable.' He also points out that 'the traditional base (of *The Bridge*) is complex' and that 'the structural pattern ... is superb.'

In his memoir of the 1920s, *Exile's Return*, originally published in 1934 and revised in 1951, another of Crane's friends, the poet and critic Malcolm Cowley, wrote that Crane was 'a poet of ecstasy, or frenzy or intoxication; you can choose your word depending on how much you like his work.' He cites that Crane was inspired by 'alcohol, jazz, machinery, laughter, intellectual stimulation, the shape and sound of words, and the madness of New York.'

Cowley also goes on to say that 'at their worst his poems are ineffective unless read in something approximating the same atmosphere, with a drink at your elbow, the phonograph blaring, and somebody shouting into your ear, "isn't that grreat!"' But 'at their best ... the poems do their work unaided except by their proper glitter and violence.' With his closing comment about

Crane's poetry Cowley reveals what he then considered one of Crane's best poems, a sequence from *The Bridge*. 'At their very best, as in "The River", they have an emotional force that has not been equaled by any other American poet of our century.' 'The River' is analysed in Part Two of this study.

In his first book of criticism, *The Double Agent* in 1935, which focused on Modernist poets and included a lengthy essay on Crane, the poet and critic R.P. (Richard Palmer) Blackmur, focused largely on Crane's deficiencies. He wrote that Crane's 'vagueness of purpose, in spite of the apparent concrete character of the Brooklyn Bridge, which became the symbol of his epic, he never succeeded in correcting.' He also gave his opinion that *The Bridge* 'suffers from a lack of coherent structure'. He rounded off his essay by concluding, on a romantically infused negative note, that 'There is about (Crane), too – such were his gifts for the hearts of words, such the vitality of his intelligence – the distraught but exciting splendour of a great failure.'

In 1951, Stanley K. Coffman jr. focused on Crane's use of symbolism in *The Bridge* in a critical essay. Coffman highlighted Crane's 'brilliant elaboration of symbolic meaning' in the sequences of the long poem, but also added that 'the brilliance is vitiated by failure to cope philosophically with his material'. So, the common charge against Crane's work – with some solid justification, especially in *The Bridge* – is the dominance of high style over a unified theme or subject. But Coffman does allow the caveat that 'one ought not attempt an estimate of *The Bridge* without understanding Crane's grasp of a fundamental Symbolist technique.'

By 1953, Allen Tate's opinion of Crane's work had also become less positive than it had been when he wrote the introduction to *White Buildings* in 1926, and his essay's title 'The Self-Made Angel' immediately alerts us to this, in that he now saw Crane as an illusionist or a magician. But isn't that what all poets are in the end, conjurers of words, to articulate meaning? Surely only those under romantic delusion or youthful naivety see the poet as only a sage or visionary, and not the precision-hewn finest word engineers?

'Crane, like most men today, was a self-made angel, trying to cheat the condition of man ... Crane put forward images of self-destruction under the illusion that they were images of an intenser spiritual life,' Tate wrote. Then he concluded faithfully, yet stealthily: 'I am not repudiating my praise of Crane. He was probably as great a poet as a magician can be.'

Fast forwarding to 1963, and in his book *Hart Crane* Vincent Quinn pointed out the fact that Crane saw himself as 'a seer' and puts him firmly in the lineage of 'Blake, Coleridge, Poe, Emerson, Baudelaire, Rimbaud.' Quinn eloquently states the inner drive of such poets: 'In this tradition the creative experience of the poet is regarded as a gratuitous visitation far beyond his conscious power and control.'

This recalls Coleridge famously being unable to complete his poem 'Kubla Khan' (subtitled 'A Vision in a Dream') as a caller at the door interrupted that undoubtedly opium-assisted dream-sleep state. But how much did Coleridge and the other major poets in Quinn's list, including Crane, honestly believe that their verse came from inspired visions, or did they know that it came from a calculated sleight-of-hand mastery of words for effect, magicians all, as Allen Tate claimed of Crane?

But it is interesting how much Quinn's reading of Crane chimes with Crane's own riposte to Harriet Monroe, quoted earlier in this study, with 'emotional dynamics' being of a higher order than 'science' in his poetry. And it is interesting that in this reader's experience, as a reader/writer, many very fine writers can be read and how they achieved their effects is discernible. But in Crane's case, this is difficult to discern. Therefore, either Crane was a greater master of his craft, or he did indeed have some unconscious, or subconscious, visionary input.

In their 1980 essay, which focuses on one of Crane's early poems from his teenage years, 'The Moth That God Made Blind', never published in a collection, Norman D. Hinton and Lise Rogers looked at the foundations of Crane's philosophy. And of course, a writer's philosophy, or way of looking both inwardly and out at the world, and asking questions, is intrinsic to all literature.

Considering the influence of the artist and writer Carl Schmitt, whom Crane befriended when he first got to New York in 1917 before his eighteenth birthday, the two critics cite how Schmitt taught Crane how moral experience and sensual experience must balance each other. For a young man dealing with sexual feelings and addressing being gay in a world then where it was seen as morally abnormal, and by many abhorrent, achieving that balance would be a feat.

But it's not all about sexuality. A poet as sensitive and as emotionally acute as Crane would already be brutally exposed to the 'good and evil' 'and beauty and ugliness' of the world, and the need to find an equilibrium. As Crane's correspondence with Schmitt and others shows, Crane was entranced by Schmitt's philosophical ideas at this time. And the juxtaposition of opposites, the friction between light and dark, would run through Crane's poetry. In that early poem, when Schmitt's influence was probably at its zenith, the plight of the blind moth in the poem's title is set in relief against the 'happier' life of the other sighted moths.

In 1996, Tim Dean, a British academic who specialises in 'queer theory' in American poetry, and did his doctorate on Crane, wrote in a critical article: 'Crane's poems instantiate a form of private experience that can be concealed no more than it can be revealed. Intensity eliminates inviolate *identity* and produces instead a second order of substantive privacy – that if inviolate *experience* – which the poems preserve for their readers. Crane's reader is asked not to identify with a textually generated subject position (homosexual or otherwise) but to reexperience a *jouissance* that eliminates every subject position.'

Finally, in his 2015 book *The Daemon Knows* the late Harold Bloom, the highly esteemed critic of American literature and Shakespeare scholar, revealed just how much he was captivated by Crane's poetry, over a long life which had seen him immerse himself in many great writers. 'Whitman, Emerson, Melville, Dickinson, and Stevens I have loved incessantly but not with the passion that Hart Crane's poetry goes on evoking in me.'

Bloom was an avid admirer of the early poems collected in *White Buildings* and of *The Bridge* and saw Crane's late poem 'The Broken Tower' as one of the poet's greatest achievements.

While it is of high quality and proves that Crane was far from being creatively spent as he, by all accounts, then thought, 'The Broken Tower' is not analysed in Part Two of this study. This is due to it being written in the final few months of Crane's life, meaning it would be the final poem examined here, and as it is despondent in tone and outlook, it would be a disservice to Crane to finish a selected review of his oeuvre with that work.

As said earlier, Crane's tragic early death has often overshadowed his poetry, and it seems fitting to end the analysis here on the high note of the poems from *The Bridge*. For while Crane was a very subtle and nuanced poet, taking in the whole spectrum between darkness and light, and of joy and despair in his poetry, he was essentially an optimistic man in his poetry, with an exultant and celebratory lyrical vision and impulse, and not the depressed figure of his last few months.

Crane's early death is tragic, in both human terms and in terms of the poetry he could have gone on to create, but the work he achieved in his life is vibrant, uniquely energetic, and life-affirming.

And as to the obscurity and opaqueness of much of Crane's poetry, and the need to invest in him as a reader, Harold Bloom was unequivocal. 'In some respects, Hart Crane is the most difficult of all American poets, but that is part of his greatness. To read him properly, you need to enhance your awareness of sound and sense in his diction, syntax, and cognitive music. In doing so you will learn to read Shakespeare better.'

PART TWO

IN DEPTH CRITICISM OF INDIVIDUAL POEMS AND SEQUENCES

From *White Buildings* (1926)

Crane had a prolific correspondence with his friend the critic Gorham Munson, and in a letter dated 6 February 1923, we can see how Crane was focused on assembling his poems already written into his first book collection. 'I hope I can get enough material together during the next few months for a small volume where things can be arranged in proper order.'

Some of these poems were already starting to appear in important literary magazines and journals such as *The Dial*, *Poetry*, *Broom*, *The Double Dealer*, *Fugitive*, *Little Review*, *1924*, and *Secession* in America, and *The Calendar* in London, England. But every poet needs a collection.

It would be another three years before that debut collection *White Buildings* appeared, published by Boni and Liveright in New York. But by the time he wrote that letter, Crane had helpfully already become friends with two nationally prominent and successful writers, Sherwood Anderson, and

Eugene O'Neill, who aided his development through writerly support and encouragement, and by their validation, they undoubtedly opened well-guarded and tightly-closed inner literary doors for him.

Crane had the early open admiration of the prose writer Sherwood Anderson, famous for the critically acclaimed and influential 1919 book of short stories *Winesburg, Ohio*, who like Crane had grown up in that state and lived in Cleveland for a time. Crane penned a laudatory review of *Winesburg, Ohio* in September 1919 in the magazine *The Pagan*, in which he wrote, 'America should read this book on her knees. It constitutes an important chapter in the Bible of her consciousness.'

After that, a correspondence started between the two men, and they became friends. And in 1921, after the magazine *The Double Dealer* accepted his poem 'Black Tambourine', which would appear in *White Buildings* five years later, Crane was commissioned to write a critical essay about Anderson, in which he singled out the writer's 'sincerity' and 'humanity' and exalted his lyrical prose.

The two men fell out, however, when they met in person in 1922, when Gorham Munson, also present, got into a literary spat with Anderson, and by which Crane, by association, was tainted, as Munson's loyal close friend. One wonders if Anderson could have helped Crane's career more if they had remained friends, just as later Anderson would help Hemingway in a sort-of-mentor capacity, and whom Hemingway would later characteristically denigrate.

Crane's friendship with the playwright Eugene O'Neill, already the recipient of three Pulitzer Prizes for drama and a

Broadway hit, managed to remain intact. O'Neill felt an affinity with Crane's poetry – as another future dramatist, Tennessee Williams, would later – and agreed to write a preface for *White Buildings*, wrote it, but then decided that he didn't feel it was good enough, so in the end the poet and critic Allen Tate provided a positive yet measured one, some of which was quoted in Part One of this study.

O'Neill did contribute an important validatory blurb for Crane's debut collection: 'Hart Crane's poems are profound and deep seeking. In them he reveals, with a new insight and unique power, the mystic undertones of beauty which move words to express vision.' Such praise from such a literary titan was a great public calling card for Crane's poetry.

And, as we have seen, the immediate critical response to the lyrical poems of *White Buildings* was generally positive, and aside from Edmund Wilson's and Harriet Monroe's marked reservations (although they both admired Crane's style), and Tate's less forthright qualms, most important poets and critics saw real potential for greatness in Crane poetry.

Five of the poems from *White Buildings*, including the six-part 'Voyages' sequence, are examined here in this study.

'Legend'

The first poem in Crane's first collection has been seen by many critics as the poet expounding and exhilarating in his sexuality, and it can certainly justifiably be read in that way. As recently as August 2022, the British poet Carol Rumens wrote in the *Guardian* that 'Legend' is 'a young man's daring and defiant assertion of his sexuality.'

But on first reading it as a young man, this writer saw it as Crane's declaration of artistic intent, an acknowledgement of his calling, a willful dedication to his poetic vocation after a prolonged inner struggle, which, in his case, was as deeply personal to him as his sexuality. We know from his letters that being a poet to Crane was as important as breathing, and as natural, and like his sexuality, at times very painful.

It is also a celebration of his poetic gifts but infused with the risks and conflicts that Crane knew, even as a young man, came with the talent that drove him. In a letter to his father C.A., Crane revealed his feelings about his talent and the difficulties that came with it. 'I have powers, which, if properly balanced, will enable me to mount to extraordinary latitudes. There is constantly an inward struggle, but the time to worry is when there is no inward debate.'

We know from the recollections of various close friends and contemporaries that Crane was very aware of his talent, and that he could be arrogant at times. But this admission of his inner conflict, in a letter to his father, the businessman who lived in the very real world, the one which his son was ill-adjusted to by gift and temperament, is a highly personal heartfelt admission.

The tension, that 'inward struggle' runs through Crane's poetry, and in fact is most probably a major factor in that poetry's creation. And it can also be linked right through to his suicide: perhaps by then Crane had given up on, or wasn't able to have, that 'inward debate' anymore. Crane was ultimately unable to achieve that 'balance' he realised early he needed to reach. The imbalance rendering emotion over a clear theme, subject, and philosophy in some of his major poems is testament to that.

Written in free verse, the first two-line stanza is very arresting: 'As silent as a mirror is believed/Realities plunge in silence by ... '

Crane immediately attacks our perceptions, of ourselves, and what is around us. With that opening, he immerses the reader in a sense of mystery and mystique, as telegraphed ahead by the poem's title.

He continues by obstinately telling us, 'I am not ready for repentance/Nor to match regrets.' Crane is refusing to apologise for who he is or make any excuses for himself. But he is honest in telling us here that he's a work in progress, setting out on his journey voyage, and that this is painful – 'this cleaving and this burning': a working through, purging of, and learning from, his conflicted emotions. This can of course be read as referring solely to his sexuality, or in a wider sense finding himself as a young man and his place in a world not made for him, or both.

And the end of the poem leaves us in no doubt that Crane has vowed to give himself to poetry and accept himself. It is also a rallying cry to others like him – 'those who step the legend of their youth into the noon.' The noon or midday sun is the brightest and most exposing, and this is a brave call to both personal and poetic arms.

'My Grandmother's Love Letters'

This is one of Crane's most simple and direct poems, and so the most accessible, with clear themes and emotions clearly linked to them. It focuses on his close relationship with his grandmother Elizabeth Hart, and for this reason it is also one of his most nostalgic and sentimental poems.

Not only did Crane and his grandmother have an almost umbilical attachment, Crane having spent an extended period living with her while growing up, but Elizabeth remained a key correspondent and confidante for years after he had left home. And Hart's strained relationships with his father C.A. and mother Grace made his connection to Elizabeth all the stronger. She was also responsible for the young future poet's first immersion in literature, as he spent many hours in her personal library devouring her collection of classics.

This is a poem about memory, the connections and missed connections between past and present generations, the desire to understand somebody you love more completely, and the realisation that some channels to the past are inevitably lost. It is deeply personal, as are all the best of Crane's poems.

'My Grandmother's Love Letters' was completed in 1919, almost seven years before *White Buildings* appeared. As his biographer John Unterecker tells us, it was rejected by *The Little Review* and then accepted by *The Dial*, a very prestigious literary magazine, which paid him the sum of ten dollars, Crane's first payment for a poem, and published it in 1920.

The language is beautiful and extremely evocative in a grand yet still modern romantic manner, and that is uniquely Crane. But the simplicity and the closeness you feel to Crane as he addresses you reminds this reader of the less ornate later work of another American poet, William Carlos Williams, for instance in his 1934 poem 'This is Just To Say'.

'My Grandmother's Love Letters' is written in iambic pentameter over six stanzas: three of four lines, and three stanzas of seven, one and six lines each. The opening, 'There are no stars to-night/But those of memory' immediately sets up a harkening back to the past and a deep need to understand it. This is caused by the poet finding a stash of his grandmother's love letters hidden in the roof of the attic of her home.

Crane conveys the fragility of his connection to his grandmother's youthful past in her love letters, when he tells us that the paper on which they are written are 'brown and soft/And liable to melt as snow'. This evokes the fact that his kinship with Elizabeth's younger emotional self is ethereal and liable to vanish and evaporate at any moment. But he yearns to understand her and feel what she felt all those years before.

He lets us know that he must tread carefully while trying to find a link to her: 'Steps must be gentle' and 'it is all hung by an invisible white hair', which is very poignant, although his grandmother was very much still alive at the time the poem was written.

The one-line stanza refrain, 'And I ask myself', sees Crane questioning his ability to reach her, asking if his 'fingers are long enough to play/Old keys that are but echoes' and 'Is the silence strong enough/To carry back the music to its source'. We feel his desperation and deep need to find that relation to her through time, and music, as it would appear in many of Crane's later poems, is key to memory and thought.

He knows what he is trying to achieve is very difficult, perhaps impossible, a forlorn desire. To touch the essence of his grandmother in her vibrant and exhilarating youth through her letters is probably going to fail, but he is determined to keep trying – 'Yet I would lead my grandmother by the hand/ Through much of what she would not understand.' Crane knows that she, like his young self in the present, wouldn't understand her emotions at the time she felt them.

But Crane is adamant that he will persevere in reaching out, to connect with his grandmother and guide her, no matter how difficult it is: 'And so I stumble'. The poem ends with the sound of the rain on the roof, 'With such a sound of gently pitying laughter.' The cold reality of the present is unremitting, but his love for his grandmother remains deep within him and the need to feel closer to her will never die.

'Chaplinesque'

Written in September 1921, soon after Charlie Chaplin's film *The Kid* was shown in Cleveland where Crane had temporarily returned to live, 'Chaplinesque' is more than merely a tribute to Chaplin and his already iconic creation, 'the Tramp'. It reveals how Crane had come to realise how art could capture and symbolise a culture and humanity – one that less than two years later he'd begin to strive to do himself in *The Bridge* – as well as being a deeply personal poem.

It is a homage to Chaplin's understanding of the American psyche, more incredible when one considers, and it's unknown whether Crane knew, that Chaplin was an immigrant born poor in Southeast London, England, just over a decade before himself.

But then Chaplin tapped into the human psyche, which attracted and still attracts universal empathy. That is 'the little guy' who gets one over on those above him, the underdog who repeatedly makes his social superiors look stupid and antagonises them, yet at the same time shows great sympathy and compassion for those even more vulnerable than himself, such as children, young ladies in distress, or animals.

The Tramp is arguably the most famous evocation of the divide and battle between the haves and have-nots in popular culture, a chance for the many who felt disenfranchised to stick an ungloved finger up at an unjust materialistic society and those they see as their oppressors: 'us and them'. It was a socialist impulse which would later help make Chaplin a major Hoover-era FBI target due to his perceived Communist sympathies, and along with the scandal stoked up by his predilection for very young women, lead to his prolonged exile in Europe.

But all that was in the future. Crane understood Chaplin and his Tramp persona to a remarkable degree, despite being just twenty-two years old when he wrote 'Chaplinesque'. This is apparent in the first stanza of the poem: 'We make our meek adjustments,/Contented with such random consolations/As the wind deposits/In slithered and too ample pockets.'

Crane sees how we futilely face our place in the world, finding cold comfort, but really at the mercy of chance and nature, the survival of the fittest. Although Crane goes on to tell us that we 'can still love the world', at least those who 'find a famished kitten' and find refuge for it from 'the fury of the street'.

This is an image which could easily come from a Chaplin film, but we know that, in this instance, Crane was channeling his own personal experience and equating it with Chaplin's

Tramp, represented best as Crane writes in the poem, by Chaplin's/the Tramp's 'pliant cane'.

But is Crane only alluding to the cane itself, the bendability of the Tramp's great prop, or is he saying that the Tramp himself is easily influenced, and at the mercy of his surroundings? The former is more likely, as the Tramp is often proactive in his actions, rather than just reactive to circumstances.

And we know from Crane's biographer John Unterecker that the poet himself had rescued a black kitten from an alley in Cleveland and looked after it for a time. And the theme returns in the poem's final stanza: 'And through all sound of gaiety and quest/Have heard a kitten in the wilderness.'

Crane tells us that we should be aware of those who require help or an ear, even in the moments when we are content and even exhilarated, or our minds and hearts enveloped and sealed by our own desires and ambitions. It's an idealistic message, and one infused with the naivety of youth, but it is also real, pure, and touching, and optimistic about human nature.

It is also a sentimental message, as the Tramp is, of course, but in a letter to his friend Gorham Munson, Crane defended Chaplin against sentimentality, writing that in the work of the great actor/director 'sentimentality is made to transcend itself into a new kind of tragedy, eccentric, homely, and yet brilliant.' And there is also a great deal of Romanticism in Crane's poetry, after all.

This need for compassion and humanity in a confusing and often cruel world is the core message of 'Chaplinesque', and one that Crane recognised in Chaplin's early silent films featuring the Tramp. But it's also a personal plea from Crane, who already knew that he was an underdog in the wider world, despite his confidence, until the last months of his life, in his rare poetic gifts.

And Crane was very aware of his place in the world at the time he composed the lines of 'Chaplinesque'. His letters show that he'd recently taken one of his several breaks from his father, a temporary estrangement at that point, as the businessman and the poet couldn't compromise on their natural instincts: money versus art, the here-and-now and posterity.

And the line in the third stanza, 'We will sidestep, and to the final smirk/Dally the doom of that inevitable thumb/That slowly chafes its puckered index toward us', shows us that Crane was opposed to the values of the capitalist world, even if he understood through practicality that he had to somehow survive within it.

Crane knew that his talent gave him power in only a rarefied niche, with very little real-world influence, and even that depended on his acceptance by others within that narrow field. It's a call for compassion and empathy, an appeal to humanity's natural capacity to feel and reach out to others, the less fortunate, the lonely, and the lost. If we empathise with others, we remain human.

And Charlie Chaplin himself read and appreciated the poem. In 1923, after it first appeared in a magazine, Waldo Frank arrived late one evening at Crane's New York apartment. The three went out to dinner, and Crane discussed the poem with Chaplin, then one of the most famous people in the world. In a letter that Crane wrote excitedly to his mother, he wrote of Chaplin's 'twinkling eyes', and that Chaplin had shared his thoughts on his own current work. Chaplin dropped Crane back home in a taxi early in the morning, before he went on to the Ritz where he was staying.

This must have been an incredible experience for the poet, and for those hours the two men seem to have connected as artists, as equals. Crane hoped that a deep friendship would ensue, but he would only meet Chaplin one more time, in California in 1927, and the occasion was not so intimate. But the fact that Chaplin approved of and understood Crane's poem about his style and influence can only add another fascinating layer to a reading of it.

'At Melville's Tomb'

This poem written in blank verse is obviously a homage to the great nineteenth-century writer Herman Melville, most famously the author of the novels *Moby Dick*, *Billy Budd*, and *Typee*, and the short story, 'Bartleby the Scrivener', although he also wrote much poetry later in life.

Melville achieved literary success in his late twenties and early thirties, a period which culminated in the publication of his masterpiece *Moby Dick* in late 1851, which failed commercially. He never regained popular appeal or financial security, was a New York City customs inspector for almost twenty years, and lived until the age of seventy-two, publishing nothing more but working on long epic poems.

Melville's struggles as a writer in the second half of his life, having already penned prose works which would posthumously become American classics, is the key to Crane's poetic tribute.

From his letters, we know that Crane first read *Moby Dick* in

1922, and it had a profound effect on him, and would continue to be a key homegrown American literary influence on the poet, through the writing of *The Bridge* and after.

In the last full year of his life in Mexico in 1931, Crane reportedly said in conversation, when he felt despondent and temporarily blocked as a writer, that Captain Ahab's monologue speeches in the novel were 'pure poetry' and he wished *he* could write like that. When his friend Lesley Simpson told him that he *could* write like that, Crane said that he could once, that *The Bridge* was good, but that 'I'll never do anything like that again.' *The Bridge* had only been published the previous year.

And in 1932, not long before his death, Crane wrote in a letter to his longtime friend Solomon Grunberg that 'In *Moby Dick* the whale is a metaphysical image of the Universe, and every detail of his habits and anatomy has the importance of swelling his proportions to the cosmic role he plays.'

This not only shows how keen a reader Crane was, but also that he was striving to learn from Melville, to find metaphor to express his themes, a vessel to frame and convey his poetic thought. He would use the Brooklyn Bridge in *The Bridge*, and that long poem has allusions and motifs of the sea running through it, as well as a river, in fact dominating some sections. And a Melville quote heads the 'Cutty Sark' sequence of that poem.

Crane had already begun devising, reading in preparation for, and composing *The Bridge* when he wrote 'At Melville's Tomb'. Like the longer poetic sequence 'Voyages I-VI' which came directly after it in *White Buildings* and is analysed next in this study, the sea has great symbolic power within its lines.

He began writing 'At Melville's Tomb' in late October 1925, so it was one of the last poems he composed which made it into *White Buildings* the following year. It was rejected by several magazines, and John Unterecker informs us that it was 'revised each time an editor returned it.'

As mentioned in Part One of this study, it eventually appeared in *Poetry* magazine in October 1926, when it had already appeared in book form, and the editor Harriet Monroe made Crane write an explanation of his poetic methods, which she published beside the poem for the benefit of readers. In that explanatory mini-essay, Crane outlined his 'logic of metaphor', the poetic use of fine-drawn imagery to represent another image; and 'At Melville's Tomb' is loaded with metaphoric symbols and hidden meanings to unearth.

It is comprised of sixteen lines in total, with four stanzas of equal length, written in iambic pentameter, with no rhyming scheme.

We are at the side of Melville's grave, offering tribute through Crane's eyes, as he sees what Melville saw – for five years as a young man, Melville worked on whaling vessels, which of course inspired *Moby Dick*, and he was briefly in the US Navy. But is the vision that Crane channels really Melville, or his most famous character, the whaler Captain Ahab?

And the sea, its power and fury, claiming those it wants or chooses, consequently dominates from the beginning of the poem: 'Often beneath the wave, wide from the ledge/The dice of drowned men's bones he saw bequeath/An embassy.'

Crane immediately makes the sea a captor, a grave, that 'embassy' of the deep, a theme which he builds on, with lines such as 'the calyx of death's bounty' in the second stanza – the calyx are the sepals of a flower, the whorl which protects the budding petals. This is a symbol for the sea as a guard of those who perished within it.

He returns to the idea of the sea as a protector at the end of the poem: 'High in the azure steeps/Monody shall not wake the mariner.'

The sea is a mausoleum, the 'monody' a reference to a poem which grieves for a dead person, as well as being an ode from Greek tragedy, vocalised by one actor. The skeletons of those who drowned at sea lie peacefully at its bottom, and no poem or song, however beautifully recited or sung, can disturb the tranquillity down there.

And the final line of the poem is intrinsically powerful – the reader, through Crane as he conveys what Melville/Ahab saw, is both awed and feels a sense of foreboding: 'This fabulous shadow only the sea keeps.'

The majesty of the ocean, and the way it cares for and shields its human dead, is celebrated, 'fabulous', but this is juxtaposed with the looming darkness of 'shadow'.

Much has been made of the fact that Crane committed suicide by jumping overboard into the ocean, and 'At Melville's Tomb' does show a marked respect and affinity for the sea as a place to lie at rest, untroubled and safeguarded by the fathoms beneath the waves. As previously stated, Crane certainly had a preoccupation with the sea as a metaphor in his poetry.

But the main thrust of this poem is a bow to Herman

Melville, from one artist to another – Crane sees the dead master writer as a martyr of literature, somebody who gave his all to art, just as Crane himself would go on to do.

Just as 'Legend', the first poem in *White Buildings*, was a promise to give himself, and sacrifice his youth and life to poetry and art, 'At Melville's Tomb' is a lament for Melville, and one written out of the most profound respect.

For a dedicated and avowed vocational poet such as Crane, there can be no greater praise for another artist than that. It also shows that Crane was aware in his mid-twenties of the emotional and practical risks he was taking in giving himself, mind, body, and soul, to poetry.

'Voyages I-VI'

This long poem in six parts is the final sequence in *White Buildings* and it is one of the individual works for which Crane is best known. He also rated it highly himself. When he was asked in 1931 – six years after the sequence appeared in his first collection, and the year before his death – to choose his best poem for the anthology *The Book of Living Verse*, Crane chose 'To Brooklyn Bridge' from *The Bridge*, or as his second choice, either 'Voyages II' or 'IV'.

Written in iambic pentameter, it had been composed over a lengthy period, and Crane incorporated earlier work into the sequence. For instance, parts of an early poem from 1921 entitled 'The Bottom of the Sea is Cruel' made it into 'Voyages I'. Crane did most of the writing of the sequence as it would ultimately appear in 1924, and in a letter late that year to his friend the novelist and poet Jean Toomer, the son of a former slave and associated with New York's Harlem Renaissance literary movement, Crane wrote, with the poem enclosed, that 'I have never been given the opportunity for as much joy and agony before.'

It is a love poem, and in its lines, Crane wears his heart openly on the page. It was inspired by the poet's extended relationship with Emil Opffer, a Norwegian sailor, and the exhilaration and turmoil of true love, that 'joy and agony' described by Crane, is powerfully evoked. Opffer would often be at sea, and he would have ten-day stopovers in New York, and he and Crane would meet for dinners and go to concerts, as well as sharing intimate moments.

The passions that Crane felt inspired some of his greatest concentrated lyricism – it's an intense poem, his feelings distilled, yet living and breathing for eternity. It is also an extremely ambitious poem, and it succeeds in capturing the frenzied emotional instability of being in love – the exhilaration, the doubts, the guilt, the desires fulfilled and thwarted. And from the beginning in 'Voyages I', Crane uses the waves and turbulence of the sea to convey his emotions, beginning with the innocence of childhood: 'Above the fresh ruffles of the surf/Bright striped urchins flay each other with sand.'

He watches the children in Victorian swimming suits playing in the shallows, as they 'flay each other with sand' without a care in the world. But then he turns to issuing a warning, telling us 'And could they hear me I would tell them'. While urging them to continue frolicking – 'frisk with your dog/Fondle your shells and sticks, bleached/By time and the elements', he proceeds to give his hard-earned advice: 'but there is a line/You must not cross nor ever trust beyond it'.

It's as if the children are safe on the shore, the water just lapping them, but Crane himself, when older, had swum too far out, allowing love to engulf him, opening himself to the downside of love's joy: pain and heartache. And the final line leaves us in no doubt that Crane's message is a cautionary counselling to those yet to emotionally commit themselves: 'The bottom of the sea is cruel.'

So by the end of 'Voyages I' we have taken a journey from the unfiltered, un-self-conscious jubilation of childhood to the young man wizened by the experience of feeling love, and the price paid to feel it. As the 'Voyages' sequence continues, this turbulent expression of what love feels like continues, and you realise that Crane really is taking you on a voyage into his heart and soul, but one that anyone who has ever felt the unpredictability and double-edged nature of true love can relate to and understand.

'Voyages II' goes on to give another view of the sea – that metaphor of love – and a much more positive one. Instead of the cruelty at the bottom of the sea, where it can be implied that dead lovers lay skeletally wrecked, now the ocean is seen as a giver of life, an opportunity for rebirth. The first two words of this section, 'And yet', after the foreboding ending of 'Voyages I' immediately tell us that Crane is viewing the sea in a different, more hopeful way: 'And yet this great wink of eternity,/Of rimless floods, unfettered leewardings … '

The duality of the sea is still there, the danger it poses hasn't gone away, but there is now the chance of being remade by love, the waves washing over you instead of the current dragging you down to the depths: 'Take this sea ... As her demeanors motion well or ill,/All but the pieties of lovers' hands.'

And there is an erotic charge in the fourth, penultimate stanza, where Crane uses the image of a flower to relay the physical as well as spiritual closeness of love: 'Hasten, while they are true, – sleep, death, desire,/Close round one instant in one floating flower.' The budded flower, that symbol of fertility and birth, is seen as floating on the sea's surface, and not devoured and sunk down below. In the image of the flower, love survives.

The final stanza ends with a plea for safe passage and guidance, but not until that love has been fulfilled, and death has been outstared. 'Bequeath to no earthly shore until/Is answered in the vortex of our grave/The seal's wide spindrift gaze toward paradise.'

We are exposed to the elements, as the 'spindrift gaze' – the sea water is sprayed from the crests of waves by the wind, an ecstatic ejaculation. But Crane looks on and does not blink and doesn't hesitate in remaining focused on his goal of 'paradise' where love will engulf him. Crane's vision of love here is idealistic and shows his faith in it after consummation, in contrast to the sea's propensity for doom in 'Voyages I'.

'Voyages III' is exultant in tone and language, with the power of the sea channeled through its use of cleansing and washing over those who encounter it, as Crane constantly does on his eponymous voyages.

Crane references Shakespeare's *The Tempest* in its exploration of the theme of 'a sea change', one of the many Shakespearean phrases which entered common English language usage, meaning a complete change or transformation, ostensibly of the soul.

In *The Tempest*, Ariel sings about Prospero: 'Those are pearls that were his eyes;/Nothing of him doth fade,/But suffer a sea-change/Into something rich and strange.' Interestingly, T.S. Eliot also used this theme in *The Waste Land*, which of course we know Crane knew well by the time he wrote 'Voyages'.

In the first section of *The Waste Land* entitled 'The Burial of the Dead', Eliot directly borrows Shakespeare's line when talking about 'the drowned Phoenician sailor' in Madame Sosostris's 'wicked pack' of tarot cards: 'Those are pearls that were his eyes. Look!'

Crane is more subtle, and his reference to Shakespeare as a source more oblique: 'but this single change, – /Upon the steep floor flung from dawn to dawn/The silken skilled transmemberment of song;' It is Ariel's song that Crane refers to here, and the sea change which is coming.

The only question is whether Crane located this connection directly from Shakespeare or through Eliot, but a poetic mind as sophisticated as Crane's undoubtedly knew that close readers would make the connection and identify both sources.

The process of this sea change or renewal and rejuvenation is Crane's vision of his voyage on the sea. This is wildly evoked by Crane in the lines 'Star kissing star through wave on wave unto/Your body rocking!', but this is directly followed by the shadow of death, but soothingly not a violent one: 'and where death, if shed/Presumes no carnage ... '

'Voyages III' concludes with Crane seeking passage on the voyage, that journey into the depths of love and change, in a final standalone line: 'Permit me voyage, love, into your hands ... '

In 'Voyages IV', Crane and his lover are in the throes of a passionate relationship – 'No stream of greater love advancing now/Than, singing, this mortality alone/Through clay aflow immortally to you.' The language is romantic and adoring, with intimate descriptions of the object of his desire and affection, such as the 'Blue latitudes and levels of your eyes, – '

And the metaphor of the budding flower found earlier in the sequence returns in the final couplet: 'In this expectant, still exclaim receive/The secret oar and petals of all love.' The oar is for progressing forward on the sea, and the petals that symbol of the budded birth and fertility of full-blown love.

'Voyages V' is particularly interesting regarding its rhythms – which like some sections of *The Bridge* (addressed next in this study) are infused with jazz. Crane is known to have listened to loud music, both classical and jazz, on his gramophone when writing his poetry in a euphoric state.

The sounds evoked here are shortened and cut-back, like jazz rhythms, quite different to the more expansive romantic sounds of the other sections: 'Meticulous, past midnight in clear rime/Infrangible and lonely, smooth as though cast/Together in one merciless white bade – /The bay estuaries fleck the hard sky limits.'

And we can tell that Crane is unsatisfied and disheartened here, his love held back, and the connection to his lover thwarted through a sense of betrayal. 'Knowing I cannot touch your hand and look/Too, into that godless cleft of sky/Where nothing turns but dead sounds flashing.'

Crane is veering between apathetic and nihilistic here, the pain of love having engulfed him, the self-doubts, and hesitations about the true nature of the bond with his lover dominating the tone of the poem.

But there is intimacy along with that despair: 'In all the argosy of your bright hair I dreamed/Nothing so flagless as this piracy.' Crane reveals to us that he feels cheated, used, his heart stolen, as if by a pirate, his heart stripped and emptied, rather than a galleon being plundered.

But the concluding section, 'Voyages VI', is more positive. Although Crane reveals his neediness and vulnerability, and the feeling of being lost in love, his vision is tinged with hope, which means that he feels that the love he feels could be mutual.

Crane calls on the highest power for help in his quest, through an invocation to the Greek goddess Aphrodite, the symbol of love, lust, passion, pleasure, and beauty. She is the ultimate power over the ocean in ancient Greek myth, as she was born of the sea.

Crane invokes her, explaining how committed he is to his quest for love on the ship's voyage, perhaps a ship like that sailed on by his lover Emil Opffer, Crane's love for whom was the inspiration for the whole sequence: 'My eyes pressed black against the prow,/ – Thy derelict and blinded guest ... '

Crane is blinded by love, and is making a plea to Aphrodite, whom he refers to as 'the lounged goddess' and whose eyes express all, making words unnecessary: 'Conceding dialogue with eyes/That smile unsearchable repose – '

This is the culmination of the 'Voyages' sequence, with Crane imploring the goddess of love to see him safely through his quest on her natural home, the sea.

From *The Bridge* (1930)

Constituting the most substantial cornerstone in the bedrock of Hart Crane's poetic reputation, this epic poem is also the work for which he is most widely recognised today.

As broached in Part One of this study, the critical reception to *The Bridge* on publication was extremely disappointing to Crane, who had laboured long and hard on its composition. Citing a reliance on obscure lyrical flights, lack of coherence, and clear themes and structure, an irony as the actual Brooklyn Bridge is renowned for the strength of its design. Influential critics, including most champions close to Crane, while pointing out some favoured high points and sections, intimated that he had lost his way in this very ambitious attempt at a major long poem.

But over time, the achievements of Crane in *The Bridge* have been more perceptibly realised, although some noted critics, such as Adam Kirsch, still see it as wildly uneven in terms of quality, Kirsch writing in the *New Yorker* magazine in 2006 that it is 'an impressive failure'. And it has never garnered the poetic-epoch-changing status of Eliot's *The Waste Land*, which preceded it by almost eight years, and to which Crane was responding with his own more positive and celebratory vision of the myth of America.

It does though have its place as one of the major long poems of the twentieth century, and in some parts of the poem Crane soared to heights of poetic accomplishment reached by few in history. At its best, *The Bridge* lives and breathes, taking the reader on a rollicking journey through time, going back centuries to the discovery of America through to the mid-late 1920s, and taking in a wide variety of its inhabitants and their dreams and realities.

And it is a positive vision of America, both its past and future. In a letter to his friend Gorham Munson as early as February 1923, when the themes and ideas for *The Bridge* were first taking shape in his mind, Crane wrote that he found inspiration all around him for his long poem of America: 'The field of possibilities literally glitters all around one with the perception and vocabulary to pick out significant details and digest them into something emotional.'

As his biographer John Unterecker summarised, Crane already knew that he 'was to discover in the American past the roots on which a future might be founded.'

In a letter to Waldo Frank fourteen months later in April 1924, when he was still very much in love with Emil Opffer, Crane's dual infatuation with the Brooklyn Bridge, near where he was living in rooms in a brownstone at 110 Columbia Heights, is very apparent, and it was presumably with Opffer that he recounts walking: 'And I have been able to give freedom and life which was acknowledged in the ecstasy of walking hand in hand across the most beautiful bridge of the world, the cables enclosing us and pulling us upward in such a dance as I have never walked and never can walk with another.'

In the same letter, Crane refers to his digs at 110 Columbia Heights in Brooklyn, writing 'Note the above address, and you will see that I am living in the shadow of that bridge.' In fact, one of the rooms that Crane was occupying was used by the supervisor of the construction of the Brooklyn Bridge, the civil engineer Washington Roebling, as a vantage point for overseeing its slow progress as it was built between 1869 and 1883. Crane later claimed that he'd had no idea of this connection until after he finished writing *The Bridge*.

The quotation at the beginning of the poem is from *The Book of Job*, the first of the Poetic Books of the Old Testament. It follows the exact wording found in the original King James Bible and the American Standard Version, and in those respective versions, the words are spoken by Satan to the Lord and Jehovah: 'From going to and fro in the earth,/and from walking up and down in it.'

The Bridge was published first in a deluxe limited edition – 283 copies, with fifty of them printed on Japanese Vellum and signed by Crane – in 1930, by Harry and Caresse Crosby's avant-garde Black Sun Press in Paris. Crane had spent some time in Paris with the Crosbys in 1929, Harry even providing Crane's bail when he was arrested for drunkenly fighting in a cafe. A few months later, *The Bridge* appeared in a larger commercial print run with Horace Liveright in New York.

Both editions contained photographs of Brooklyn Bridge by the now-renowned American photographer Walker Evans. Just over a decade later, Evans would make his name with his collaboration with the writer James Agee on their photo-reportage classic of tenant farmers and their families living in poverty in the American South during the Great Depression, *Let Us Now Praise Famous Men*.

Crane put everything he had into *The Bridge*. In a 1927 letter to his then patron, Otto Kahn, in his own words the poet reveals the scale of his ambition and investment in the long poem: 'Each section of the entire poem has presented its own unique problem of form, not alone in relation to the materials embodied within its separate confines, but also in relation to the other parts, in series, of the major design of the entire poem. Each is a separate canvas, as it were, yet none yields its entire significance when seen apart from the others. One might take the Sistine Chapel as an analogy.'

The Bridge consists of fifteen sections, and a selection of five of them are examined here.

'To Brooklyn Bridge'

A prelude to the epic sequence, the first poem that makes up *The Bridge* introduces the majesty of the huge physical structure of that feat of engineering, which as we know from his letters, so awed Crane. It also acts as an introduction to the themes of the whole long poem, and how Crane will examine stratas of human life, and the history and myth of America.

Written in iambic pentameter free verse, Crane does however use rhyme four times in the eleven four-line stanzas: rhyming 'away' and 'day' in the third and fourth lines of the second stanza; 'scene' and 'screen' in the second and fourth lines of the third stanza; 'clear' and 'year' in the second and fourth lines of the tenth stanza; and 'sod' and 'God' in the second and fourth lines of the eleventh stanza. This is interesting, as it shows Crane playing with strict form, and playfully experimenting with his use of often tightly controlled and traditional poetic structures.

The first stanza sets the soaring lyrical tone, as he describes the Brooklyn Bridge looming over New York's East River, connecting Brooklyn and Manhattan: 'How many dawns, chill from his rippling rest/The seagull's wings shall dip and pivot him,/Shedding white rings of tumult, building high/Over the chained bay waters Liberty – '

This sets the scene wonderfully, the seagulls flying and diving over the cold metal of the impressive bridge, an epic presence, and as such the springboard to Crane's imagination, where his eponymous poem will be anchored as he travels through time and America in the rest of the poem. And the juxtaposition of the 'chained bay' with all that the Statue of Liberty represents – freedom and hope, one of the very foundations of (the fallacy) of the American Dream – is highly effective.

And after we have settled into the mythic aura of the bridge and what it represents – a pathway to the rest of America, its history, myth and identity, Crane injects some contemporary-to-him late 1920s modernity into his lines in the third stanza: 'I think of cinemas, panoramic sleights/With multitudes bent toward some flashing scene.'

It's a strong image of people leaning forward rapt by a film, perhaps a Chaplin silent, as Crane himself immortalised in his earlier poem 'Chaplinesque'. The visual image is one of Crane's great strengths, and *The Bridge* is abundant with such rich and evocative imagery.

Then the fifth stanza takes us to the reality of any high bridge, the fact that it attracts those attempting or committing suicide: 'Out of some subway scuttle, cell or loft/A bedlamite speeds to thy parapets,/Tilting there momentarily, shrill shirt ballooning,/ A jest falls from the speechless caravan.'

The jumper is before us, out of their mind or insane – 'a bedlamite', an old-fashioned term for a lunatic, after the infamous London asylum Bedlam. Having left their home and taken the subway/underground train, climbed high up on the bridge, we witness this poor man or woman teetering on the edge of the hard and cold iron beneath their feet, their shirt blowing up in gusts of wind. Is that a joke or laughter coming from this desperate, now nihilistically apathetic person? Or is 'the jest' from the millions below who can't hear them, or perhaps don't want to hear, and would say nothing?

By the final stanza, using an Elizabethan poetic style, 'O sleepless as the river under thee', Crane takes us back to the magnitude of the bridge, linking its presence with both myth and God.

'Ave Maria'

This was completed in the summer of 1926, when Crane was enmeshed in a frenzy of writing on the Isle of Pines, a French-governed island in New Caledonia. He soon sent a draft copy of 'Ave Maria' to his mother Grace, writing: 'Here is the first section of *The Bridge* – Columbus meditating at the prow on the return from his first trip – he thought he had found the way to India, you know.'

And that is where 'Ave Maria' takes us, back to Christopher Columbus's accidental discovery of America in 1492, while trying to find a direct route from Europe to Asia (ostensibly 'Cathay' or China), now on his voyage back to Spain. So, from the wonder of modern engineering of 'To Brooklyn Bridge', we are transported back more than four centuries to when America was given its name in the post-Columbus era.

Columbus speaks directly to us from the first stanza, as he stands at the bow of his ship and rehearses what he will say to Queen Isabella I of Spain (along with her husband King Ferdinand II the voyage's sponsor), and Juan Perez, whom Crane explains in a side note were 'two faithful partisans of his (Columbus's) quest.'

'Be with me, Luis de San Angel, now – /Witness before the tides can wrest away/The word I bring ... /I bring you back Cathay!'

We also get the real sense of danger and uncertainty felt by Columbus and his crew aboard the Santa Maria, and those all who sailed on the two other smaller vessels the Niña and the Pinta faced – 'Here waves climb into dusk on gleaming mail;/ Invisible waves of the sea, – locks, tendons/Crested and creeping, troughing corridors/That fall back yawning to another plunge.'

Crane evokes Columbus's great religious faith and the deep belief of his times, referencing God, Isaiah, the Garden of Eden, and the connection between it and the sacred mission of his quest: 'White toil of heaven's cordons, mustering/In holy rings all sails charged to the far ... '. We can sense that Columbus and his men 'know' that they are in the hands of a higher power as they are tossed around on often violent seas.

Columbus's challenge is conveyed by Crane at the end of 'Ave Maria', in a rising crescendo, the lines of which are written haphazardly on the page, a stark contrast to the mostly eight-line stanzas of the rest of the poem: 'And kingdoms/naked in the/trembling heart – /Te Deum laudamus/O Thou Hand of Fire.'

The Latin phrase 'te Deum laudamus' translates as 'God, We Praise You' is an early Christian hymn of praise, and one which would have been very much in use in the late fifteenth century, and this is undoubtedly why Crane selected it to come from Columbus's mind and mouth.

And the declaration 'O Thou Hand of Fire' is possibly inspired by the Prologue of Shakespeare's *Henry V*, in words spoken by the chorus – 'O for a Muse of fire, that would ascend ... ', and later includes the line, 'The perilous narrow ocean parts asunder.'

This seems a fitting finale for Columbus, standing on the foredeck, taking confidence in God to give him and his crews safe passage back to Spain. And Crane has given *The Bridge* the historical grounding it requires to truly encompass the sweep and breadth of American history and attendant myth.

'The River'

As a boy, Crane travelled extensively between 1908 and 1916 from their home in the Midwest. Between the ages of nine and seventeen, he journeyed with his mother Grace through America's West, the Pacific Northwest, and Canada, and these extended trips and the sights he saw on them fed into the landscape and imagery of *The Bridge*, and especially 'The River'.

As Unterecker points out, Crane sold a poem entitled 'The Great Western Plains' for a dollar to *Gargoyle* magazine in the summer of 1922, and he would reuse much of the material from that poem, but enhancing it, when he composed the final version of 'The River' five years later in June 1927.

Crane sent a copy of 'The River' to his father C.A. soon after its composition, and C.A. responded positively and sympathetically, though with a characteristic eye on commerciality. C.A. wrote back that the poem was 'the best I have ever seen of your work. When I say the best it more nearly approached that low standard which I could understand. Something of this nature, in my humble opinion, would sell better than other things I have seen; it does not leave quite so much to the imagination.'

Crane is known to have read sections of *The Bridge* aloud to friends when it was in draft, and one can imagine that 'The River' would have been quite a reading. The speed and inflections would have been modulated, but surely with the jazz rhythms which permeate it, the reading would have been fast in parts, conveying the sheer exhilaration and crescendos of the writing as we are swept along in a torrent from its opening lines: 'Stick your patent name on a signboard/brother – all over – going west – young man/Tintex – Japalac – Certain – teed Overalls ads/and lands sakes! under the new playbill ripped/in the guaranteed corner – see Bert Williams what?'

We are travelling west across America on a train, shooting past the contemporary 1920s advertisements on hoardings – Tintex (fabric dye); Japalac (a Prohibition-era cocktail); Certainteed workman's overalls; and a performance by the popular vaudeville entertainer Bert Williams, who was born in the Bahamas before moving to the US, and was the first Black man to play the lead in a film (Williams had died in 1922).

Crane gives us a vivid snapshot of the era as we embark on a whirlwind journey. The margined and unnecessary explanatory note he gives us, ' ... and past the din and slogans of the year – ' confirms what we are reading.

And the pace of the rhythms is unrelenting – the soundtrack in the reader's mind is pure jazz, from New Orleans to blues to Jazz Age. Crane makes use of partial-capitalisations of words to enhance the syncopation and flow of the lines:

> ... and whistling down the tracks
> a headlight rushing with the sound – can you
> imagine – while an EXpress makes time like
> SCIENCE – COMMERCE and the HOLYGHOST
> WALLSTREET AND VIRGINBIRTH WITHOUT STONES OR
> WIRES OR EVEN RUNning brooks connecting ears
> and no more sermons windows flashing roar
> breathtaking – as you like it ... eh?

And with the next lines, Crane introduces the tramps or as they were called then in American vernacular 'hobos' who feature prominently in 'The River' – 'So the 20th Century – so/ whizzed the Limited – roared by and left/three men, still hungry on the tracks ... '

These men represent the past, still living a downtrodden and near feral existence, despite the great advances of the early twentieth century – in science; the capitalism and pervading influence of 1920s Wall Street; while 'virgin birth' is very likely a sly reference to the 1921 British case of the clairvoyant Christabel Russell, whose husband John denied paternity of her baby, and the scandal that ensued when it was revealed that during pregnancy, Christabel's hymen had been unbroken.

The affair attracted international headlines, especially in the United States.

Crane opens a window for us on a transient and impoverished stratum of rural American society in the early twentieth century, which stands in contrast to metropolitan New York which infuses much of *The Bridge*, and particularly 'The Tunnel' section, which is examined next in this study. Crane endeavours to give us 'all' of America, past and his 1920s present, in the entirety of *The Bridge*.

'The River' is the gateway to the journey through America, taking in the various aspects of its heritage, history, the attendant myths, and the people who have inhabited the vast country.

As Crane himself wrote in a 1927 letter to his Aunt Sally, 'I'm trying in this part of the poem to chart the pioneer experience of our forefathers – and to tell the story backwards as it were, on the "backs" of hobos. These hobos are simply "psychological ponies" to carry the reader across the country and back to the Mississippi, which you will notice is described as a great River of Time.'

Crane's Aunt Sally is referenced in 'The River', when members of a road gang are talking to each other, and he sought her permission to include her name, which was granted.

'I heard a road gang chanting so./And afterwards, who had a colt's eyes – one said,/"Jesus! Oh I remember watermelon days!" And sped/High in a clod of merriment, recalled/"And when my Aunt Sally smiled," he drawled – /"It was almost Louisiana, long ago."'

And the reference to his father C.A.'s factory – where the

poet had worked – shows us just how Crane absorbed and remembered all that was and had been around him: 'Behind/ My father's cannery works I used to see/Rail-squatters ranged in nomad raillery,/The ancient men – wifeless or runaway/Hobo-trekkers that forever search/An empire wilderness of freight and rails.'

We travel on, through the Ozarks and past Iron Mountain, Ohio, Tennessee, down to the Mississippi, and finally the Gulf of Mexico. Along the way history and legends seep into the lines, and by the end of 'The River', the reader feels as if they have taken that long North American journey, mile after mile, through the country and time.

This section of *The Bridge* is one of Crane's crowning achievements. No poet, including the ecstatic Walt Whitman, a definite influence on Crane, has ever reached the level of sheer manic energy, yet controlled meaning, contained in the lines of 'The River'. Reading it is exhilarating, and its effect doesn't dissipate over time.

Malcolm Cowley, whilst he had reservations about *The Bridge* as a poetic entity when reviewing it, was certainly justified in writing that 'The River' was 'one of the important poems of our age.'

'The Tunnel'

Written in the summer of 1926, 'The Tunnel' uses the New York subway/underground train system to convey and powerfully bring the colour, darkness and light of that city and its inhabitants alive.

Other major American poets had set poems on subway and

underground train networks since the beginning of the twentieth century – Ezra Pound in Paris and William Carlos Williams in New York – but Crane's 'The Tunnel' is the one which truly brings the feeling of murky, crowded, and claustrophobic subterranean travel to life.

And Crane wrote from experience, from travelling on the New York subway. In a letter to his friend the theatrical designer Richard Rychtarik in August 1926, Crane wrote: 'Work continues. "The Tunnel" now. I shall have it done very shortly. It's rather ghastly, almost surgery – and, oddly almost all from the notes and stitches I have written while swinging on the strap at late midnights going home.'

Almost exactly a year later, Crane was thrilled when none other than T.S. Eliot validated his poetry. Already seen as the pre-eminent poet of his generation, and whose *The Waste Land* had done so much to inspire *The Bridge*, Eliot asked if he could publish 'The Tunnel' in *The Criterion*, the literary journal he edited, which in 1927 was briefly a monthly, rather than a quarterly, publication.

Crane switches poetic metres repeatedly in 'The Tunnel' and utilises free verse. This adds to the immediacy and urgency of the lines, and like the previously examined section 'The River', it flows fast and with great intensity. The speed of reading fluctuates, and the first half of 'The Tunnel' is a rapid outpouring, and accessible, the second half is more measured and the language more opaque. But the overall effect is both seductive and startling.

The quote at the beginning of 'The Tunnel' is from William Blake's poem 'Morning': 'To Find the Western path/Right thro' the Gates of Wrath', and this is fitting, as we are travelling and constantly moving as we read, trying to reach the destination where Crane is taking us.

The opening lines immediately thrust us into the city of New York at nighttime, as the narrator of the poem makes his way through the well-lit streets and dark alleys, making his way down into the subway to go home. And Crane encapsulates both the bustle and life of the city and the darkness and danger in the first lines of the first ten-line stanza:

> Performances, assortments, résumés –
> Up Times Square to Columbus Circle lights
> Channel the congresses, nightly sessions,
> Refractions of the thousand theatres, faces –
> Mysterious kitchens ... You shall search them all.

Crane's repeated use of 'you' in direct address to the reader includes us and draws us straight into the action and into his experience. And by the end of the stanza, the hazards of the city at night appear, and like him, Crane knows that we would like to be cosily tucked up in bed, with the only danger near us the crime reports in the newspaper: 'Finger your knees – and wish yourself in bed/With tabloid crime sheets perched in easy sight.'

And then there is the only indented part of 'The Tunnel', as Crane pulls us into the boisterous milieu further, as if he's guiding us: 'Then let you reach your hat/and go./As usual, let you – also/Walking down – exclaim/to twelve upward leaving/a subscription praise/for what time slays.' The use of 'also' adds to the frenetic atmosphere, as if we have a lot to take in around us as we go about everyday actions, such as walking down into the subway to catch the train in the tunnel. Crane is taking us underground, beneath the city.

And Crane's imagery is masterful, as he evokes the tension of the people waiting for the train, the use of 'you' once again including us – 'But you find yourself/Preparing penguin flexions of the arms, – ' Has there ever been a better evocation of the physicality and mindset of people and place?

The poet also uses rhyme very effectively in 'The Tunnel', enabling a rhythm to build, and giving the reader the ability to recite the lines rapidly, as he tells us to hurry through the crowds: 'Be minimum, to swim the hiving swarms/Out of the Square, the Circle burning bright – /Avoid the glass doors gyring at your right,/Where boxed alone a second, eyes take fright/ – Quite unprepared rush naked back to light ... '

We are right there with Crane as he gets onto the train, and as it pulls away through the tunnel. He overhears conversations, and one can imagine these have blossomed from snatched snippets he himself had heard on his nightly travels home in the early-mid 1920s.

Other standout images jump out at the reader, such as 'and love/A burnt match skating in a urinal – ', which is such a profound insight into the pain, desperation, and disappointment of love which dies, all hope washing away, slowly, like that matchstick whirling around in the disgusting stink of a public toilet. Likewise, the cleaning lady 'with the bandaged hair' he sees sitting on the train is brought to life before us. This is descriptive writing of the highest standard.

The darkness and near-terror of the lives of the city's night commuters in their moving train snaking through the tunnel out towards New York's outer boroughs and eventually suburbs are also elicited in the second half of 'The Tunnel'. Several references to the demon that drives these people to take this cavernous journey repeatedly at night and in the early morning: 'And does the daemon take you home also ... ?'

Finally, the train goes back overground, and we encounter 'A tugboat, wheezing wreaths of steam.' Back above the surface, Crane ends 'The Tunnel' with 'Kiss of our agony Thou gatherest,/ O Hand of Fire/gatherest – '

This of course recalls and links back to the way the earlier 'Ave Maria' section of *The Bridge*, examined earlier in Part Two, ends with the line 'O Thou Hand of Fire'. In 'Ave Maria', it's Columbus who is imploring and praying for God's aid with those words, while in 'The Tunnel,' the 1920s commuter – Crane, the others riding the subway trains, and through them, us the readers – who are still searching, for meaning, direction, and help in our confused lives.

'Atlantis'

This is the concluding section of *The Bridge*, but it was in fact the first part that Crane wrote in early 1923, and as such it was the creative seed which grew into the epic poem. It is formally and tightly constructed, comprising of twelve eight-line stanzas, although less formally, some are randomly rhyming, and others completely non-rhyming.

The quotation from Plato at the beginning of 'Atlantis' was of course as always carefully chosen by Crane – 'Music is then the knowledge that which relates to love in harmony and system.'

The aptness of this quote is that it was Plato in his 350 BC dialogues *Timaeus and Critias*, who was the first ever to write of the myth of Atlantis. Plato invented the fictional island of Atlantis in this work, describing it as a major naval power and threatening geographically close rival 'Ancient Athens', itself a utopian construct of Plato's mind. But when the actions of those on Atlantis upset the Greek Gods, especially Neptune, the island sank deep into the Atlantic Ocean and was lost forever.

Crane makes full use of this myth, and we can see how it continues the obsession he felt about the sea, symbolising love, death, and rebirth, as we have seen earlier in this study, most notably in his 'Voyages' sequence of poems from *White Buildings* and the 'Ave Maria' section of *The Bridge*, in which Columbus and his crews sailed the Atlantic Ocean.

And as the critic Alfred Corn succinctly put it in a 1985 critical analysis of 'Atlantis', 'For Crane, the Atlantic serves as a link between America and Europe, between the active present and the contemplative or visionary past.' The ocean surrounding New York's harbour, just like the Brooklyn Bridge, are key gateways to America, and to Crane's poetic imagination and *The Bridge*'s structure.

The eminent critic Harold Bloom, as mentioned earlier in this study a devoted longtime admirer of Crane's work, wrote that 'Atlantis' is not Crane's most perfect poem, but that it is his 'icon' and that 'all of his dangerous gifts come together here.'

From the first stanza of 'Atlantis', the modernity and wonder of the Brooklyn Bridge's unique architecture and its cabled arcs is celebrated:

> Through the bound cable strands, the arching path
> Upward, veering with light, the flight of strings, –
> Taut miles of shuttling moonlight syncopate
> The whispered rush, telepathy of wires,
> Up the index of night, granite and steel –

And then Crane eulogises the river beneath the bridge, which of course eventually runs into the Atlantic Ocean. He expertly juxtaposes the modern engineering with the timeless quality of the water below – 'And through that cordage, threading with its call/One arc synoptic of all tides below – /Their labyrinthine mouths of history/Pouring reply as though all ships at sea ... '

The connection between America's past and future is made explicit with the line ' – Tomorrows into yesteryear – and link/ What cipher-script of time no traveller reads.' And the river or its source the sea, is a lifeforce; and those who travel on or above it drowned by its power, which is full of love and death: 'But who, through smoking pyres of love and death,/Searches the timeless laugh of mythic spears.'

We also have two references to 'Cathay', which was first introduced when Columbus was speaking in the 'Ave Maria' section of *The Bridge*, meaning China. Likewise, the 'Hand of Fire' seen in both 'Ave Maria' and 'The Tunnel' returns in the last lines of 'Atlantis''s final stanza as the 'Bridge of Fire'. Crane gathers the threads of *The Bridge*: ' – One Song, one Bridge of Fire! Is it Cathay,/Now pity steeps the grass and rainbows ring./ The serpent with the eagle in the leaves ... ?/Whispers antiphonal in azure swing.'

The reference to 'the serpent with the eagle' comes from *Aesop's Fables*, where an eagle is attacked by a serpent and is being overwhelmed, until a man frees the eagle. In revenge, the serpent puts its venom in the man's water, but the eagle knocks the water out of the man's hands before he can drink it, and he is saved in return.

The moral of this fable is that 'an act of kindness is well repaid.' Crane here is ending 'Atlantis' and *The Bridge* on a positive note, expressing the need for altruism and respect by humans for nature and other human beings, and by doing so, America will continue to make progress and have a glorious future, which is of course in total contrast to the negative feelings about humanity and the modern world in Eliot's desolate masterpiece *The Waste Land*.

The finality of Atlantis in the poem serves as both a synthesis of the thematic strands explored in the sections of *The Bridge* leading up to it – and tellingly, as mentioned earlier, it was composed first – but it's also full of confusion and questioning. It is as if we are in Crane's head, exploring his inner mind, which is made real on the page.

And it is the climax of Crane's true magnum opus, *The Bridge*, being an incredible achievement, the one for which he will be forever judged. Five years before *The Bridge*'s publication, T.S. Eliot famously wrote to F. Scott Fitzgerald that *The Great Gatsby* was to his mind 'the first step American fiction has taken since Henry James.'

Eliot was of course American himself, but aside from *The Waste Land*, which inspired Crane – and Eliot's epic poem was written in England and has a distinctly European temperament – it could also arguably be said that *The Bridge* was the first real step American poetry had taken since Walt Whitman.

BIBLIOGRAPHY

Primary Sources

Crane, Hart; Brom Weber (editor) *Complete Poems* (Bloodaxe Books, Newcastle, 1987) (Includes Weber's Introduction to the 1966 *Complete Poems* and Waldo Frank's foreword to the 1958 edition)

Crane, Hart *The Letters of Hart Crane 1916-1932* (Berkeley: University of California Press, 1965)

Secondary Sources

Books

Bloom, Harold *The Daemon Knows: Literary Greatness and the American Sublime* (Spiegel & Grau, New York, 2015)

Cowley, Malcolm *Exile's Return: A Literary Odyssey of the 1920s* (Viking Penguin, New York, 1951)

Fisher, Clive *Hart Crane: A Life* (Yale University Press, 2002)

Hamilton, Ian *Against Oblivion: Some Lives of the Twentieth-Century Poets* (Penguin, London, 2003)

Mariani, Paul *The Broken Tower: The Life of Hart Crane* (W.W. Norton & Company, New York, 2000)

Quinn, Vincent *Hart Crane* (Twayne, Boston, 1963)

Unterecker, John *Voyager: A Life of Hart Crane* (Anthony Blond Ltd, London, 1970)

Articles & Essays

Blackmur, R.P. 'New Thresholds, New Annotated Notes on the Text of Hart Crane', *Direction* magazine 1935

Coffman jr., Stanley K. 'Symbolism in *The Bridge*', *PMLA*, 66 Modern Language Association of America, 1951

Corn, Alfred 'Hart Crane's "Atlantis"', *Southwest Review*, Summer 1985 Southern Methodist University

Dean, Tim 'Hart Crane's Poetics of Privacy' *American Literary History* 8:1 Spring 1996

Foster, Edward Halsey 'Gay Literature: Poetry and Prose', *Oxford Research Encyclopedia*, 2017

Frank, Waldo 'The American Jungle' (from the 1933 essay 'Hart Crane') (Farrar & Rinehart, New York, 1937)

Hinton, Norman D., and Rogers, Lise 'Hart Crane's The Moth That God Made Blind', *Papers on Language and Literature*, (Southern Illinois University at Edwardsville, 1980)

Hutchinson, Percy (initialed P.H.) 'Hart Crane's cubistic poetry in *The Bridge*' (Review of *The Bridge* on publication) *New York Times*, 27 April 1930

Tate, Allen 'Introduction to *White Buildings* by Hart Crane', (Boni and Liveright, New York, 1926)

Winters, Yvor, 'The Progress of Hart Crane', *Poetry* magazine June 1930